Praise for A. C

'We are mystified, alarmed, even frightened by the cascade of events that beset our world. A. C. Grayling not only clarifies the way in which these events are challenging the workings of democracy – amid the rise in populism in response – but comes up with solutions.'

Jon Snow, journalist and broadcaster on *Democracy and Its Crisis*

'Grayling incisively surveys attempts by Western thinkers, from Plato and Aristotle to Madison and Tocqueville, to resolve what he calls the "dilemma of democracy": the tension between the belief that power belongs ultimately to the people, and the desire for stable and humane government.'

Wall Street Journal on *Democracy and Its Crisis*

'An enthusiastic thinker who embraces humour, common sense and lucidity.'

Independent on *For the Good of the World*

'A must read for anyone with questions, worries and fears about pollution, poverty, protectionism, populism, weapons proliferation, and where our world is headed.'

Gordon Brown, former UK prime minister on *For the Good of the World*

'Grayling is particularly good at illuminating the knottiness of moral discourse.'

The Sunday Times on *For the Good of the World*

Also by A. C. Grayling

The History of Philosophy
The Future of Moral Values
What Is Good?
Among the Dead Cities
Against All Gods
Towards the Light
The Choice of Hercules
Ideas that Matter
To Set Prometheus Free
Liberty in the Age of Terror
The Good Book
The God Argument
The Age of Genius
Democracy and Its Crisis
The Good State
The Frontiers of Knowledge
For the Good of the World
Philosophy and Life
Who Owns the Moon?
Discriminations

FOR THE PEOPLE

Fighting Authoritarianism,
Saving Democracy

A. C. GRAYLING

ONEWORLD

A Oneworld Book

First published by Oneworld Publications Ltd in 2025

Copyright © A. C. Grayling, 2025

The moral right of A. C. Grayling to be identified as the Author of this work has been asserted by him in accordance with the Copyright, Designs, and Patents Act 1988

All rights reserved
Copyright under Berne Convention
A CIP record for this title is available from the British Library

ISBN 978-1-83643-144-2
eISBN 978-1-83643-143-5

Typeset by Geethik Technologies
Printed and bound in Great Britain by Clays Ltd, Elcograf S.p.A.

No part of this book was written with AI.

No part of this publication may be reproduced, stored in a retrieval system, or transmitted, in any form or by any means, electronic, mechanical, photocopying, recording or otherwise, or used in any manner for the purpose of training artificial intelligence technologies or systems, without the prior permission of the publishers.

The authorised representative in the EEA is eucomply OÜ,
Pärnu mnt 139b–14, 11317 Tallinn, Estonia
(email: hello@eucompliancepartner.com / phone: +33757690241)

Oneworld Publications Ltd
10 Bloomsbury Street
London WC1B 3SR
England

Stay up to date with the latest books, special offers, and exclusive content from Oneworld with our newsletter

Sign up on our website
oneworld-publications.com

MIX
Paper | Supporting responsible forestry
FSC® C018072

CONTENTS

Preface   ix

Introduction   1

1 'Of, by, for' the People   9
2 High Finance and Democracy   34
3 The Alternative Model: Turning to Authoritarianism   74
4 Interference Undermining Democracy   107
5 Restoring Democracy   144

Appendix I   175
Appendix II   178
Notes   218
Index   257

'We ought to have our government so shaped that even when in the hands of a bad man we shall be safe.'
Frederick Douglass (1818–1895)

PREFACE

Are we living through the end of the democratic moment in history? Democracy, so recently acquired, less than two centuries old at the uttermost and still not available to a large portion of the world's population, is under pressure. Many are losing faith in it; others are working to undermine it. This book examines the reasons why this is so and how it is happening, and offers solutions – or at least ameliorations – because what democracies give their peoples in the way of civil liberties, human rights and the rule of law is too precious to lose. It is therefore vital to save the constitutional system that embodies them.

It is important at the outset to note that the term 'democracy' applies to a spectrum of constitutional arrangements, gathered under this name because they share a common basis in the principle that sovereignty in a system of government lies in the expressed consent of the people. There is a second assumed but not often articulated principle implicit in this idea, namely, that government exists, or should exist, for the benefit of the people. Both these principles require clarification; as stated in these general terms they admit of different interpretations, and the interpretations matter. When used in an unqualified general sense, the term 'democracy' in the following pages denotes a polity explicitly resting on the first principle, viz. that government derives its legitimacy from 'the express consent of the people' – a phrase which itself requires explanation.

In earlier books aimed at a general readership I used 'democracy' in the sense of the first principle, leaving to context the development of a view about which form of it is to be preferred, justifying that preference by appeal to the second principle, viz. that government exists for the benefit of the people, 'people' here meaning every individual in the state.[1] Those books were written under the pressure of circumstances, when significant events in the year 2016 prompted a starker sense of threat to democratic orders posed by how the world had evolved in the course of preceding decades, especially in economic and technological respects. In this present book, as circumstances have worsened, some of the yet deeper matters at stake are discussed in order to make fully explicit the threats to democratic polity and what is needed to protect it and the rights and liberties it embodies. Doing so, to repeat, is hugely important: it is existential: everyone needs to be clear about the issues. Discussing them cannot be left to academic journals and theoreticians alone, but must be brought back to the centre of public debate.[2]

The primary focus of attention in these pages is the United States and the United Kingdom, and by direct implication

PREFACE

every system based on the 'Westminster model' which, in more or less adapted forms, exist in more than fifty polities (the US itself, to the surprise of some perhaps, being one). But although features of this model have a particular role in prompting disaffection with democracy, in being organised to limit the influence of the popular voice on public policy, all democracies face difficulties because of their incapacity to meet the challenges confronting them in today's world. These challenges, and ways to respond to them, are the subject of this book.

INTRODUCTION

There are four main reasons why democracy is under pressure – indeed, under attack – and why faith in it is being lost.

One is that it is not delivering enough for people's aspirations and needs, but has become trapped in political divisions and partisanships that reduce its responsiveness to social and economic diversities. Political culture in almost all democracies has become a swamp of destabilising polarisation, quarrels, untruth and propaganda, infecting the credibility of government and alienating populaces. And in a number of these cases the problem is exacerbated by systemic reasons, namely, electoral systems and the way power is located in the structure of the polity, which together dilute the effect of popular interests on the actions of government.[1]

The second reason is that multinational business lies outside the powers of single states and causes harm that democracy cannot control. Particularly over the last half-century, capitalism has produced entities too large and powerful for national governments to constrain, and its profit imperatives relentlessly drive environmental and human depredations that make citizenries despair of remedy. Accordingly, but only partly with justification, citizens blame their own polities' system. Moreover, capitalism has become a structure in which vast amounts of wealth are accumulated in fewer and fewer hands, wealth which is sequestered into tax havens depriving national economies of significant revenues, driving inequalities and empowering super-wealthy individuals and corporations to exert influence over governments, influence aimed at ensuring the protection of business activities and profits. One of a number of particularly exacerbating aspects is the arms industry and trade, a huge international business whose profits depend on the occurrence and continuation of conflict both civil and international.

The third is that the model for how polities are best organised, which in the decades after the Second World War saw many states, especially newly independent former colonies, adopt democracy in actuality or in form, no longer persuades, with China and other similarly organised authoritarian polities as – for too many in politics and business – an attractive alternative model.

The fourth is that there is deliberate undermining of democracies by anti-democrats and anti-democracies, employing interference, misinformation and propaganda, powered by the new technologies of mass and targeted communication through mainstream media and particularly social media.

Alongside these there are correlative pressures. Migration, whether prompted by poverty, conflict or climate change, feeds into domestic political pressures, and is exploited by

INTRODUCTION

populist politicians. All three of the climate, migration and conflict harms are associated with the second reason above, namely, the impunity of large multinational business.

Saving democracy matters because its benefits, obscured by these challenges, are too important to lose. These benefits are taken for granted to such an extent that they have become nigh invisible to their beneficiaries. Even though there are few places where 'true' democracy exists – most democracies are 'republican' dispensations, in the sense of this term that denotes partially-constrained elective political elites – their general conformity to principles of the rule of law, civil liberties and individual rights is a precious achievement, historically very recent and hard-won.[2] Inattention to the practical value of this achievement, and chronic disaffection with governments over matters of immediate economic and social concern within election cycles, blinds people to what they stand to lose if democracy fails. And what they stand to lose are their individual freedoms, the protection of rights and the rule of law.

Matters have reached such a point that even some of the *virtues* of democracy are perceived as failings. Democracies are noisy because of debate, argument, criticism and differences of opinion over alternative courses of action. When these turn toxic, as they have done especially over the decade and more before this writing, they seem full of endless trouble, even tumult. By contrast tyrannies are silent, apparently without political strife and disagreement because these are suppressed. Tyrannies are silent as wastelands are silent: wastelands of rights and liberties, where debate and criticism are not allowed, dissent crushed, the population a conscript army in service to a cabal or an individual. In democracies individual rights and liberties are bought at the cost of noisy striving. The false desire for political peace – for a cessation of the noise and relief from the tiring responsibility to engage – makes the apparent order of more authoritarian dispensations attractive.

This has become more so because the prime example of such a dispensation, the People's Republic of China, has learned to distract attention from actual suppression by means of bread-and-circus, consumerist, modernised-seeming arrangements enabled by high levels of economic growth – and this, for many, suffices. For not only do such arrangements distract from the absence of fundamental freedoms, but they make many people disinclined to seek such freedoms if doing so means effort and trouble. For if one conforms and obeys one can safely, even happily, get on with life, enjoying the standard of living achieved; who needs a right to express opinions about government when one's standard of living is satisfactory? Such is the thought.

Passivity of this kind might be attractive at the individual level, but conformism, suppression of alternative views, hostility to innovation and creativity (except in the technologies that serve the economy: these of course are encouraged), absence of debate, denial of intellectual freedom and artistic expression which challenges norms, result in a stultified, static, monochrome society, whose shallowness and banality crushes the spirit of anyone not insensible to the thought that because human flourishing – in any sense other than economic

INTRODUCTION

security – is a highly various matter, individual freedom matters. For all the failings and difficulties of democracies otherwise, they largely succeed in protecting individual freedoms, whose price is far beyond all that is provided by the false peace of passivity and the absence of onerous responsibilities to think, choose and participate.

It is said that 'the price of liberty is eternal vigilance'; this might better be adjusted to 'the price of liberty is eternal engagement'. In fully authoritarian dispensations the message is: 'Don't bother your heads with matters of government, and anyway if you do you will be locked up.' In democracies the message is (or should be): 'Bother your heads with government, because if you don't you will be oppressively, and in crucial respects badly, ruled over against your will.' The fact that too many cannot be bothered in the required way gives an invitation to those who wish to replace democracy with authoritarian or more authoritarian government, so that the bothered become bothered enough, one last time, to vote for their gaolers – which, in essence, is the story of populism, the movement that seeks to make a 'one last time' use of democracy to destroy democracy.

This book proceeds as follows. Chapter 1 addresses what the concept of 'democracy' in principle means, and what it means in practice. The way democracy has fallen victim to the negative aspects of politics is one reason for loss of faith in it; how this has happened – together with recent proofs of its happening – is described, and the remedy for it explained.

Chapter 2 discusses the way capitalism has metamorphosed from an effective and rational system for aspects of economic activity into an unconstrainable monster that has damaged the planet's environment and promoted inequality, injustice and both civil and international strife. If this account is motivated by any specific socio-political standpoint, it is a social democratic one premised on concessive views about mixed economies provided that the arrangements fully respect human rights, civil liberties and the aim of social justice, which are demonstrably the chief promises of the Enlightenment achievement and the most important reason why democracy matters. But a left-wing perspective does not have a monopoly on this view of capitalism; even from a centrist or moderate-conservative one the dangerous excesses of capitalism are intolerable, and demand to be called out.

Chapter 3 discusses the alternative models of governance inclined to forms of authoritarianism, and invokes both contemporary examples and the lessons of history to illustrate why, from the key standpoint of fundamental individual rights and freedoms, they are so undesirable. The discussion involves the profoundly important concept of the rule of law, examined in this chapter therefore, and why this in turn is an *ethical* matter. Authoritarianism consists in denial of the rule of law; the rule of law protects rights and liberties; the antidemocratic rise of authoritarianism is accordingly a serious threat. This is a key issue.

Chapter 4 discusses deliberate interference, especially from external agencies, aimed at undermining democracies. Although both the goal and the activity of destabilising regimes have always been a weapon on the dark side of diplomacy and international relations, the advent of the internet

INTRODUCTION

and especially social media platforms has weaponised this activity far further and with far greater effect. Addressing the problem in this new and dangerous form is a matter of urgency.

Chapter 5 gathers, summarises and concludes the points made in the preceding chapters, constituting the recipe for saving democracy in order to save the inestimable benefits it bestows in the way of fundamental rights and freedoms, given that these are what have made the best aspects of the modern world possible: science and its positive applications in medicine, economic activity, communications and quality of life, and not least the freedom to make individual choices about life, love and self-expression.

The realisation that humanity is still at an infantile stage is among the more dispiriting sentiments prompted by a survey of the state of the world. We still go to war – actually *kill* each other and any bystanders who get in the way – to resolve disputes and differences. We still not merely allow but encourage and even admire the quest for wealth, a quest too often manifesting as greed, and the celebrity wealth buys, too often manifesting as narcissism. The maturation of humanity requires what democracy promises to provide if, to use James Madison's phrase, it is 'well-constructed', namely, the full application of individual human rights and freedoms and their correlative of social and economic justice. For this we need to construct democracy well – more accurately: we need to *re*construct democracy well, because its current architecture no longer adequately sustains the promise implicit in it. The needed reforms are practicable; this is not a call for revolution. The guiding principle of reform has to be that a refreshed architecture serves the end of making democracy not just *by* the people but genuinely *for* the people – all of them, individually and collectively.

1

'OF, BY, FOR' THE PEOPLE

Perhaps the most concise, and certainly most memorable, definition of democracy was given by President Abraham Lincoln in his address at Gettysburg on 19 November 1863, in the middle of the American Civil War, at the memorial service for the many who had fallen in the fierce and bloody battle that had taken place nearby, a turning point in that appallingly wasteful conflict. Lincoln described the Union side as defending 'government of the people, by the people, for the people'. It is a splendid encapsulation of the democratic ideal. It is simultaneously a remarkably dishonest description of democracy in America not only at the time, but before and ever since; and this applies to democracy almost everywhere likewise. This is because the word 'people' has a different sense on each occurrence in the Lincolnian definition, and the equivocation lives on.

'People' in 'government *of* the people' means *everyone* in the state: men, women, children, old, young, slave, free, disabled or whole.

'People' in *by* the people' means 'those who are enfranchised, i.e. have a vote', which is not everyone but (in Lincoln's day) only *white males* and (in our day) adults aged eighteen and over not otherwise disqualified (e.g. in the UK by being peers or prisoners). But even in the latter supposedly 'universal adult franchise' arrangement, enfranchisements are not equal. The very wealthy have a 'vote' that the ordinary citizen does not have, by way of influence on political processes. Too many have a vote that can be manipulated by orchestrated misinformation and misdirection to make choices that are not in their best interests. Political government chooses which votes to notice and which to ignore. Voting systems such as 'first past the post' deprive millions of votes of any influence whatever. So the '*by* the people' people are at most a subset of the '*of* the people' people, and even then some of this subset have a super-vote and many have a vote which does not count at all.

'People' in '*for* the people' in practice and principally means that part of the people who vote for or donate money to the political party which, commanding a majority in the legislature, forms the government; for, aiming to retain power by being re-elected, a political party in government will generally ensure that its policies do not alienate its supporters, but rather will offer and implement policies that attract and retain their support. Given that even in the purest form of a democratic electoral system a party needs only fifty-one per cent to rule, 'the people' thus privileged in '*for* the people' will only at best be half the people denoted in '*of* the people'. But because of the way electoral systems work, most notably in plurality (first-past-the-post) systems, which tend always to produce two-party binaries, governments typically get the support of thirty-five to forty per cent or at most forty-five per cent of actual votes cast (thus, perhaps, twenty-five to thirty-five per cent of the total electorate, in turn perhaps less than twenty-five per cent of the total populace), so the '*for* the people' people are considerably less than half – at best – of the '*of* the people' people (i.e. everyone).

Reflection on these equivocations over the word 'people' is educative. The '*by* the people' part is key, because it is the answer to the question, 'On what does the legitimacy of government rest?' In democracy the source of power in the state is, technically speaking, the people collectively, though this both in practice and theory has come to mean the majority of the collective. In a small community – a village, say – literally everyone could be involved in debates and decisions. Variability in human psychology tends to throw up 'natural leaders', or demagogues, or people loved or admired, or who are or seem wise, and as a result even small collectives have a tendency to defer to the direction of one or a few among them. But we can indulge a Rousseau-like fantasy of pure democracy at the small scale, and locate in the collective engagement of all the people, and in particular in consensus among them, the legitimating factor in their self-government.

As a result of populations increasing in size and diversity, it becomes impracticable to gather all the people in a single place to debate and decide. This is one of the reasons for 'representative' institutions, delegates (conveying a constituency's wishes) or plenipotentiaries (acting on behalf of a constituency) substituting for the collective, or at least that part of it enfranchised to appoint them. This latter form of democracy constitutes what is more accurately called 'republicanism' or 'republican democracy' (chosen representatives acting for the *res publica* or affairs of the state). This is a rational solution to the large-population problem. The ultimate source of legitimacy still lies with the '*by* the people' people – that is, the enfranchised – who send and can recall the representatives.

But as the institutions formed to carry out governmental functions in this 'republican' version of polity come to have powers, and as elected and appointed officials of those institutions come to exercise those powers in ways too complex and numerous for direct intervention by the people, so the source of legitimacy becomes more remote from the actual performance of government, restricted to election times only – and thereby becomes increasingly notional in practice. Those professionally engaged in manning the institutions of government accordingly come to have a degree of impunity only constrainable at the margins of their terms of office – usually, the periodic election times – and even then either the invisibility or the 'spinnability' of most of what they do, submerged in the depths of detailed daily exercise of power, reduces their actual accountability.

These points are intimately related to the first reason – mentioned in the Introduction – for disaffection with democracy: that it is not delivering enough for people's aspirations and needs, but has become trapped in political partisanships that reduce its responsiveness to social and economic diversities.

'OF, BY, FOR' THE PEOPLE

The effect of the *for the people = for donors and supporters of the winning political party* aspect of the matter is very largely to blame. As franchises extended and numbers of voters increased from the mid-nineteenth century onwards, so political parties had to become more organised and disciplined in order to capture the levers of government to get their agenda through – what is known in American parlance as 'machine politics', that is, 'party machine' politics. A major result has been the explicit politicisation of government. Debates in legislatures are party political combats, showing how politics has in effect taken the place of government in at least all the headline issues and problems requiring action in any present moment of a state's life.

To say that *machine politics* has replaced *government*, or has so far infected government as to generate mistrust of government via mistrust of politicians, is to acknowledge that a danger described by Madison in his Federalist Paper No. 10, namely, that 'factionalism' (i.e. party politics) would usurp or poison government, has come to pass.[1] When the people see bitter party divisions over issues affecting their society and economy, and when they see public policy privileging one side in the debate without sufficient sensitivity or accommodation towards other sides and interests, disaffection with the whole process grows.

A significant part of the problem here relates to the question of 'the majority' – more accurately: the fallacy of majoritarianism, namely, the belief that democracy is about what the majority want, and that the majority preference therefore decides the issue. For one thing, there is no such thing as a majority. Society is a congeries of minorities (including individuals: minorities of one), enough of which can be temporarily aggregated on certain occasions in relation to a particular matter – elections, or referendums if the choice is binary – to give the illusion of 'a majority'. For another, the idea of a democratic order turns on concepts such as the rule of law, individual rights and civil liberties which, far from privileging majority preferences, explicitly exist to protect minorities and individuals from other minorities and individuals, and from any majority that aggregations of the two latter might constitute.

The fiction of 'a majority' is used when licence is required for a decision to be reached. It is a useful fiction, to an extent, because in practical affairs too much going round the houses of competing opinions is eventually counterproductive. In this respect appeal to the concept is efficacious in default of anything better. But it has come to be inflated into something it is not, viz. *the* putative source of legitimacy for the polity's institutions and practices. *The majority* is not this source; *the collective as a whole* is. *The majority* (insofar as any such thing exists more than temporarily and issue-dependently) is *only part of the collective* – indeed might only be fifty-one per cent of the collective – which is why questions of rights, liberties and the protection of law are so important, in the interests (in this case) of the forty-nine per cent – indeed again: in the interests of even one sole member of the collective.

With very few exceptions, democracies are in practice *republican* democracies in the sense noted above. Republican democracies are those in which the enfranchised part of the people elect representatives to a legislature, these representatives not mere delegates charged with conveying voters' wishes, but empowered to take decisions and enact policies on behalf of the people – all the people, not just the enfranchised.

Republican democracies are not, as common understanding now often has it, polities without kings and queens, but include constitutional monarchies such as exist in the UK, Sweden, the Netherlands, Spain, Australia, Thailand, New Zealand and Japan, in which the head of state (serving as the 'dignified' not the 'efficient' part of the constitution, to employ Walter Bagehot's distinction)[2] has no executive powers but is a figurehead merely. These monarchs are not elected to their positions but inherit them. Defenders of constitutional monarchy argue that this makes for continuity above the political fray, and a focal point for patriotism and national identity. Critics argue that, at least in some cases such as the UK itself, they perpetuate class distinctions and inequalities and are unduly expensive.

Some countries have elected Presidents who are largely or wholly ceremonial in the same way, providing the final formal symbolic step of signing laws and international treaties into effect – Germany and Ireland are examples.

Executive heads of state such as the Presidents of the US, Russia, France and Turkey also fill the ceremonial role when occasion demands, but more importantly have actual governmental powers. In the US and France the relation of the presidency to the other arms of government is more complex than in Russia and Turkey, where the presidential power is more monarchical and less constrained.

There are few examples of *direct* democracies, in which the enfranchised part of the population decides public policy by referendum. Switzerland and Lichtenstein are the only nation states with this system; in the US some New England towns have 'town meetings' to decide on local issues, while in California (notably) and about twenty other states of the Union referendums are held for a variety of reasons, including citizen-initiated proposal of laws, amendments to the state constitution, vetoing of legislative acts, and recall and replacement of elected officials.

A major reason for the establishment of representative systems is the impracticability of direct democracy for national government because of the size of the population. But another reason is that the construction of this system has, deliberately or as a result of (consciously guided, usually) factors involved in its evolution, aimed at avoiding direct democratic influence on government, not least to prevent majority oppression of minorities and individuals, and to provide a buffer between government and the chances of bad choices by voters.

A prime example of a deliberate effort in this direction is the Constitution of the US, whose framers were keen to ensure that those who legislate and govern should be fit persons possessing, to use Alexander Hamilton's phrase, 'qualities adapted to the station'; which is why in particular he proposed the idea of an Electoral College for choosing the President, a proposal accepted by the constitution framers with little dissent.[3] He and they wished to see a selected group of people, exemplifying 'information and discernment', choosing the supreme magistrate of the land, having 'taken the sense' of the popular will, which, however, they could ignore if – indeed especially if – the popular will favoured an unfit person.

Even on a cursory survey of the US arrangements one can see how the popular vote is successively filtered out of impact on the uppermost branches of federal legislation and government. Whereas in almost all US states elections for county sheriffs and judges of lower courts, and the use of referendums, instantiate a pervasive degree of local democratic participation, at the federal level the arrangements are purposely far more 'republican' than 'democratic'. The House of Representatives is elected on a plurality system, itself undemocratic (see below). The Senate seats two Senators from each state irrespective of the population of the state; it is a states' house, with great powers, and because the smaller states tend to be considerably more conservative than highly populous states such as New York and California, it is a bulwark against too-progressive policy (explaining Gore Vidal's satirical characterisation of the US as, to paraphrase, 'a country with two right-wing parties').

And finally there is the Electoral College, technically empowered to reject the outcome of the popular vote completely if that outcome is support for a person it considers 'unfit'. But today the College is in practice a rubber stamp for the party machine in each state, its members acting simply in line with the vote in their own state, having in any case been appointed in line with that state's political tendencies. The elections of Donald Trump in 2016 and 2024 are dire examples of the failure of Hamilton's intentions for the Electoral College. This is not an opinion but a matter of public fact; Trump is not merely a manifestly unfit person for public office, but a convicted felon, and a man of proven and persistent dishonesty.

The framers had what they regarded as good reason to install filters against popular will. They agreed with Plato's famous animadversions against democracy in the eighth book of his *Republic*, namely, that 'the people' are insufficiently informed and reflective, too short-term and self-interested in their preferences, too fractious and too susceptible to demagoguery, for good government to emerge from their choices. The framers accordingly arranged matters so that the institutions of the polity should work in the people's real interests when these diverged from what the people took to be their interests. This amounts to a degree of paternalism; it is a version of what Plato had argued for in the sixth book of the *Republic*, namely, that the state should be governed by 'philosopher-kings', by an elite – itself a version of 'aristocracy' ('rule by the best').

The framers of course hoped for a civic-minded people who would be conscientious in casting their votes, informing themselves, listening to debates about policy choices, and keen, as a united body, to promote the health and success of the nation inclusively. But they were realistic; as Madison argued in Federalist Paper No. 10, if the choice lies between hoping that the people would be ideal for democracy or, alternatively, raising institutions that would function to translate their imperfections into good government, one should plump for the latter. 'The inference to which we are brought', he wrote, 'is that the *causes* of faction cannot be removed, and that relief is only to be sought in the means of controlling its *effects*'; which he argues is achieved by constructing a *republican* (not directly democratic) polity, in the sense of 'delegation of the government ... to a small number of citizens'.[4] Given that his argument was aimed at promoting federalism, with the highest levels of government superior to the constituent states, his hope was that the scale of the arrangements would by itself ensure that the effects of 'the violence of faction' would be filtered out of those levels.

The structure is accordingly designed to harvest the 'consent' – not the actual choice – of the people by means of a partially democratic choice of the three arms of the polity, these being legislature, presidency and Supreme Court. The partial democracy of this last is a function of its appointment by a part of the first arm (the Senate) and the second (the President), the President nominating justices and the Senate confirming or rejecting the choice.

This structure is also designed to provide checks and balances between the three arms of the polity, the aim being to ensure thorough examination of public policy proposals, to promote compromise and achieve consensus as often as possible, and to prevent any one arm having undue power. The ambition to get good outcomes from checks and balances depends upon the different arms collaborating with goodwill in at least most decision making, otherwise the refusal of one element to collaborate will result in paralysis. As events have proved, the binary nature of US factionalism – party politics – has too often had the latter result. Repeated crisis and near-crisis over agreeing a federal budget is a familiar pattern in Washington politics.

And this result is the product of two major problems with US arrangements. One is the use of plurality (first-past-the-post) voting for the House of Representatives; the other is the failure to maintain a separation of powers between the political process and the judiciary, especially the Supreme Court and appeal courts, whose justices are political appointees.

Plurality voting produces two-party politics, squeezing out all other parties. In the US the Republicans and Democrats occupy all the political space. Together with gerrymandering – the geographical arrangement of voting districts (constituencies) into shapes conformable with their political demography – seats rarely change hands; over ninety per cent of House of Representatives seats are the permanent possession of one or other party. Two-party politics potentiates bitter divisions, the extreme of factionalism, reducing the political process to the condition of strife, infecting and hampering government.

The undemocratic nature of plurality voting is easy to demonstrate. Suppose ten people put themselves forward for election by a hundred voters. Suppose eight of them receive ten votes each, one receives nine votes, while the tenth receives eleven votes. The tenth is therefore sent to the legislature, representing eleven voters' choices while the other eighty-nine voters are unrepresented. In the generality of cases the usual outcome of plurality voting in almost all systems employing the method is that about sixty per cent, frequently more, of voters are unrepresented in government, or represented powerlessly. The system is intrinsically undemocratic. The UK is an egregious example of this: a party can secure government on a significant minority of votes cast – on numbers of registered voters at time of writing a party could theoretically win a parliamentary majority despite losing the popular vote by the huge margin of 23.7 million votes should they win by a single vote in 326 constituencies but lose by 73,200 votes to zero (73,200 being the average UK constituency size in 2019) in 324 constituencies.

The second problem, the political nature of the higher judiciary in the US, is as great a scandal as plurality voting, given the supreme importance to the rule of law that judges should be independent. It is sufficient to mention a salient recent example; the refusal of a Republican-dominated Senate to allow President Barack Obama to appoint a justice to the Supreme Court when a vacancy occurred in the last year of his second term, followed by the appointment of three justices of known Republican affiliation (and at least two widely criticised for being of dubious quality) by President Trump, giving the court a strong rightward majority. The overturn of *Roe v. Wade*, the decision to grant presidential immunity, and the licensing of a state to exclude certain voters from the electoral roll, followed. Appointments to the federal appeal courts and the Supreme Court are for life, so these appointments have a long-term effect on society. Stacking them on party political grounds is an assault on every principle embodied in the concept of the rule of law and is a characteristic of authoritarian states.

A third problem can be added to these two, arising from the role of the Electoral College in elections to the presidency. Because of the oppositional political binary generated by plurality voting, the entrenchment of political ownership of the voting base, and the fact that the rubber-stamping choice made by the Electoral College does not reflect the popular vote in the country at large, it is standardly the case that the outcome of presidential elections turns on a small number of voters in a small group of 'swing states' – in the 2024 election these were Arizona, Georgia, Michigan, Nevada, North Carolina, Pennsylvania and Wisconsin. Given the economic and military might of the US, this means that a small number of swing voters in a few and generally smaller states hold the balance of the world's fate in their hands. In the US presidential elections of 2000 and 2016 the winner had a minority of the popular vote, and the resulting presidencies prompt serious reflection on what 'alternative histories' might look like had they not been in office.

Taking these considerations together, questions arise about what the framers of the US Constitution did. All but Madison among the most prominent framers came to have serious doubts themselves.[5] Yet the Constitution has come to have the status of holy writ, in some cases to the benefit of the US people, enshrining freedom of expression and rights to due process (e.g. the First and Fifth Amendments), in others markedly less so – a stark example is the Second Amendment 'right to bear arms', adopted when 'arms' were muzzle-loading muskets with which school massacres would be difficult to effect, but very far from suitable in an era of automatic high-velocity assault weapons. This Amendment also illustrates the labile nature of interpretation: different Supreme Courts have read it in different ways, some saying and some denying that the right applies to individuals rather than militias. Given that the former interpretation has been dominant, the result in the scale of harm caused by gun ownership should be a call for a sanity check, but the profound political divide in the US makes this impossible. In 2023 there were over 600 mass shootings (eleven a week on average; 'mass shooting' is defined as occurring when four or more people are killed), and a total of nearly 43,000 deaths from gun violence – 118 a day, five an hour, one every twelve minutes.[6] In the same year in the UK there were twenty-eight deaths by gun violence, which would equate, scaling for population size, to 140.

The questions that arise focus on a dilemma. On the one hand, the framers' reasons for choosing a republican form of polity over one in which democracy is more direct are persuasive. On the other hand, the structure they devised has not worked nearly as well as they hoped. It has resulted in a deeply divided, highly unequal, violent, crime-ridden, self-obsessed society, in which corruption is as prevalent as anywhere else. That it is a society located in an immensely rich economy, with all that this implies for military prowess and world status, is attributable in part to the constitutional structure, through the opportunity it provides for entrepreneurship and the accumulation of wealth because of the freedom individuals have to engage in both. But a larger part of the reason for its economic success is its wealth of natural resources, which enabled it to achieve a dominant position in world trade after the First World War and maintain it ever since, together with other significantly conducive factors such as e.g. policies on labour rights – the general weakness of labour bargaining-power ensures labour mobility and productivity levels that suit its businesses well. The US has some of the best educational institutions in the world, while being among the worst for low levels of educational attainment overall (one in five adults is illiterate; fifty-four per cent have attainment levels below sixth grade, i.e. eleven years of age);[7] it has some of the best medical services in the world, but they are so expensive that one person in eight cannot access adequate medical care (over 25 million people);[8] it has the largest number of billionaires (twice as many as the next ranking country, China: 813 versus 406 in April 2024 according to *Forbes*),[9] while more than one in ten citizens live below the poverty line.

Economic success generates further economic success. When money is available for investment in research and technological development, when business is powerful enough to make deals internationally and domestically that suit it well, when those who are economically successful influence government, such success is guaranteed. The majority of the US population benefits from this in many ways. The whole society also pays a heavy price in the respects listed, as a divided, unequal, too violent society.

These contradictions prompt the thought that if one remains persuaded by the republican idea, then its institutions have to be modified to make the society more inclusive, less divided, more equitable, promoting a wider distribution of its economic and social goods, thus addressing factors at the root of its current problems with the aim at least of ameliorating them. This is the proposal to be advanced, explained and defended here.[10]

In the UK the original presence of counterbalancing forces between Crown, Lords and Commons has been progressively altered to place ultimate sovereignty in the House of Commons. In the House of Commons, note; not in 'the will of the people', whose 'consent' rather than any act of direct democratic legitimation is the constitutional resort of the Commons' claim to its unconstrained possession of power. How this happened is instructive and is as follows.

Limitation of the power of the Crown began with the settlement of 1688 when Parliament assumed the authority to say who will wear the Crown and took wholly into its own hands control of the national finances. Prior to 1688's 'Glorious Revolution' the doctrine by which England's kings claimed to rule was 'divine right', then a relatively recent idea given that earlier kings, in the medieval period, ruled by suffrage of the barons as in effect 'first among equals'. Given that the ruling class was literally an extended family by descent and intermarriage, quarrels over who should be king were family quarrels, a fact that explains much of the civil strife that affected England in the medieval and Tudor periods. As power increasingly centralised in the Crown because of wars with France (themselves beginning as family quarrels; the royal and aristocratic families of the two countries were related) and the increased need for taxation to pay for them, a different entitlement to kingship became necessary, and the 'divine right' doctrine was invented accordingly. But in ejecting James II from the throne in 1688 and inviting William of Orange to replace him, Parliament took the place of the deity and assumed the Crown's powers – the 'royal prerogative' as the powers are collectively known.

The next step was an accident of these events; when in 1714 Parliament invited Elector George of Hanover to be George I of England – this to keep the Stuarts out of the succession because they were Catholics – the fact that he could not speak English meant that his Cabinet conducted the business of the state with little interference (and still less knowledge) from the king, and this set a trend which, despite the muddling of George III and the occasional touch or attempted touch on the tiller by Queen Victoria, increasingly removed the Crown from affecting policy.

With the Crown out of the way, the Lords were dealt with next, in the Parliament Act of 1911, a messy affair prompted by the Lords' interference with a Budget passed by the Commons. The latter had in any case been growing in power because of successive extensions of the franchise during the preceding century. The government of the day threatened to make the king create as many new peers as would ensure passage of the Budget through the Lords; the Lords, horrified at the thought of their blue-blooded upper echelon status being diluted by the arrival of so many socially inferior individuals, gave way. This might not be the only occasion on which class snobbery served a more general interest, but it is certainly a salient one.

The position of the Lords was further diminished, practically to zero beyond some delaying and revising powers over non-finance bills, by an Act of 1949 modifying the 1911 Act to prevent the Lords from blocking the Labour government's nationalisation programme and Budget.

By this evolution the doctrine of the 'sovereignty of Parliament', recalling that 'Parliament' once meant Crown, Lords and Commons assembled together, has now come to apply exclusively to the Commons.

Left inexplicit was and is the fact that the concept of the sovereignty of the Commons and the concept of the putative final authority of the voters are in apparent tension with each other. But the appearance is illusory; 'sovereign' means 'final authority', and the Commons is sovereign. The fiction that the Commons represents, via its election by voters, the 'democratic will' of the people, is maintained for cosmetic purposes, but in fact what the voters' participation in elections at most means is that they express their *consent* to be ruled by Parliament. By accepting – because not scrutinising and challenging – the unrepresentative nature of the electoral system, 'the people' are assumed to have given their consent by not complaining about that system. But in fact, Parliament has never actually needed their consent via the ballot box; this is demonstrated by John Locke's remarks in his *Second Treatise of Government* (1689), a document justifying the Glorious Revolution, that Parliament rules 'by consent of the people', a remark made when elections to the House of Commons were vastly further from being democratic even than they are today, not least because the Lords, ruling by inheritance, was in effect more powerful since its members controlled so much of the Commons through 'pocket boroughs' – thus, seats in the Commons they literally owned.

The clinching point in the matter of Parliament's sovereignty is this. The electoral system gives majorities in the Commons (almost always on a minority of votes) which, except in relatively rare circumstances, are unassailable. The executive is drawn exclusively from this majority, and consists of the party leadership and its appointees from among supporters in the chamber. The party system is such that control of the majority vote in the Commons is exercised by the party's leadership through a system of strict party discipline. In sum this means that the executive controls the Commons. Whereas in theory the legislature holds the executive to account, in practice it is the creature of the executive. Thus the sovereignty of Parliament means the sovereignty of the executive – that is, of the party leaders. Barely considered, this is no different from what happens in authoritarian regimes.

The incorporation of the European Convention on Human Rights (ECHR) into UK law in the Human Rights Act of 1988 (effective from 2000) is unpopular with those, mainly on the right of politics, who see it as impinging on the sovereignty of Parliament. They not only wish to repeal it, but to withdraw entirely from the ECHR. The practice of 'judicial review' of administrative acts was disliked by most of the same critics for the same reason, and came to a head when in 2017 the UK Supreme Court ruled against the government's claim that it could use its 'prerogative powers' to initiate withdrawal of the UK from the European Union without further discussion. The court ruled that it could do so only with an Act of Parliament. (A Bill to the required effect, a few lines long, was hastily drawn up in the early hours of the morning after the Supreme Court decision, and as hastily passed.)[11] As a result the government passed a new Act in 2020 preventing judicial review being (in the words of the minister who introduced it) 'abused or [used] to conduct politics by other means' – in translation, 'to prevent judicial review impinging on the sovereignty of Parliament'. Such checks on the otherwise unconstrained power of Parliament – in practice, remember, the executive – as they anyway rather minimally are, given their vulnerability to the sovereign Parliament's dislike of them when under conservative control, are thus under threat (*vide* the Human Rights Act) or further diminished (*vide* judicial review).

These considerations show that the constitutional nature of the UK is at best republican if not actually party-dictatorial or oligarchic, in a somewhat extreme version because it amounts to virtually unconstrainable rule by a small political class consisting of the leadership of whichever of the two political parties (which, courtesy of the voting system, jointly occupy almost all the political space in the state) currently has its hands on the levers of power. Indeed one conservative Parliamentarian and jurist, Lord Hailsham, explicitly described the British system as an 'elective dictatorship' in his Dimbleby Lecture of 1976, on this basis urging reform of the governing institutions via a codification of the constitution.[12]

One wrong reason for dissatisfaction with democracy arises from a common mistake, which distracts from real issues about politics, government and constitutional questions. This is the failure to distinguish between 'undemocratic' and 'unrepresentative' in talking about institutions of state. Every institution of state whose existence is licensed by and adjunctival to the central institution regarded as representative (where 'representative' means 'elected', even if this goes no further than 'consented to' as with the House of Commons in the UK and the House of Representatives in the US), is *ipso facto* 'democratic' in the common usage of this term. Thus the House of Lords in the UK, and the Senate in the US, are 'democratic', as are the civil service, 'quangos' (quasi-governmental appointed bodies), police and armed services in the UK, and the executive offices staffed by presidential appointment and the police and military in the US. But although 'democratic' in this sense, they are unrepresentative, not having been elected to their positions by any constituency of the people.[13] Discontents attack such bodies on this ground, mistakenly as we see.

It is inevitable that there should be institutions of government whose legitimacy is *derived* in this way rather than *directly conferred*, given that it would be highly impracticable to elect every private soldier, every junior civil servant, every functionary engaged in carrying out some aspect of the state's business. Each such is ultimately accountable through the hierarchy of responsibility to the elected body, as it in turn is held to be ultimately accountable to (the consent of) the voters.[14]

'OF, BY, FOR' THE PEOPLE

The right reason for disaffection with democracy is the way republicanism – as the only form of democracy, or rather quasi-democracy, practicable in a populous state – has been captured by factionalism and thereby turned into oligarchy. An exacerbating factor is that a concomitant of this is that politics has become a *career*, a profession. This means that individual politicians, relatively few of whom come to hold actual power as executives, owe too much to the party to which they belong. They come to represent not the people who elected them but, instead, the party line, because doing so is what gets them elected and keeps them elected. A politician who goes against the party line and thereby loses its support inevitably loses his or her seat. There are hardly any independents in party political systems. So far has the conceit of party loyalty gone that a politician who crosses the aisle is as much likely to lose the trust of voters outside the legislature as former allies (and new comrades) within it.

Adherence to a 'party line' is not only an imperative for individual politicians concerned about their careers but is a fetish of the executive itself. Parties offer manifestoes at election times and have to appear to deliver them if they gain office. Internal disagreements, realities that derail their manifesto aims, the need to appear both consistent and in control, make parties in power (and even when out of power) engage in much dissembling and 'spinning'. A 'U-turn' on policy is considered a worse failure than telling lies. Media outlets – once almost exclusively the printed press and television news and current affairs programmes – upholding the noble myth of holding power to account but as much if not more driven by attracting customers, so that the difference between 'the public interest' and 'what interests the public' become blurred, are eager to pounce on divisions within parties and to punish U-turns as if changing minds in response to facts were an evil. Given that political parties and governments are collections of human beings, at best not much less fallible and partial, no less finite in their intellectual powers than most others, and certainly no less egoistic, they are fertile hunting ground for the media. Only the strictest exercise of party discipline keeps political parties appearing to be unified, as individual differences of opinion and individual ambition yeast away under their surface. The effect of this is to remove politics and government even further from the people and their interests.

Imagine a situation in which representatives to a legislature are independent of party-line constraints. In such a situation every measure proposed in the legislature would have to pass, if it passes, on its merits, not because a majority is 'whipped' through the lobbies on its behalf under the constraint of party discipline. In party political control of government it is not even necessary for representatives to know what the contents of a proposed Bill are; it is enough that they are expected to vote for it. They are lobby fodder. Appearances apart, what happens in Beijing's National People's Congress of the People's Republic of China (here 'the people' in both cases are only *of the people* people) and what happens in the Parliament of the United Kingdom are scarcely different.

What is the remedy for the way the republican systems of the US and UK – and by extension most 'Westminster model' systems – have degenerated in the ways described? The answer, already more than hinted, is reform of the constitutional provisions governing the institutions. That is the topic of chapter 5.

2

HIGH FINANCE AND DEMOCRACY

The view that multinational business has assumed a form over the last half-century that is endangering democracy is no longer a plaint made only by those on the left of politics, but has gone global.[1] The Covid pandemic and government actions to protect economies from the effect of lockdowns, needed to prevent wider spread of infection and fatalities, has stripped the last masking layer off the *reasons* for growing inequalities in wealth – and therefore its influence over governments and societies – by nakedly and almost instantaneously accelerating the size of the inequality gap not just between rich and poor countries but between the rich and everyone else within countries.

One effect of the pandemic was to increase the wealth of billionaires in the US by close to $640 billion to a total of more than $3.5 trillion, the largest gainers being owners and investors in the technology sector – social media companies, providers of conferencing platforms, and digital retailers such as Alibaba, Amazon, JD.com and Pinduoduo.[2] Oxfam says that the ten richest people in the world doubled their combined net worth in the pandemic, putting more into their hands than the combined wealth of the 3.1 billion people at the other end of the scale.[3] But the pandemic leap of billionaire wealth was not a new phenomenon, it was merely a sharp acceleration of a trend that has been rising steeply since 1980. In the period since that year, US billionaires have increased their wealth by 1,130 per cent, which is over 200 times more than the rise in median wages; in the same period their taxes, measured as a percentage of their holdings, dropped by seventy-eight per cent.[4] These are staggering figures.

What happened in the 1980s to trigger this process? A major factor was the implementation of ideas that underlay 'Reaganomics' in the US and were adopted elsewhere, notably in the policies of Margaret Thatcher in the UK. Ronald Reagan became president in 1981, and his policies reversed the consensus that had arisen after the First World War, and especially under F.D. Roosevelt in the 1930s, that government has an important economic role to play in society, by regulating markets to guard against excessive fluctuations that could cause collapses such as the 1929 Wall Street Crash and subsequent Great Depression, and by investing in public programmes and providing welfare to soften capitalism's harsher effects on those less able to benefit from it.

Reaganomics was a response to the 'stagflation' which by the 1970s had brought a slowdown to the US's post-Second World War economic boom. It consisted in deep tax cuts, lower social spending, more military spending, and deregulation of markets and financial services. The theory was that regulation and government spending was a barrier to incentives in business and interfered with the operation of markets. Reagan therefore lowered taxes and cut spending on Social Security, Medicaid, Food Stamps, education and training. Just one example of the effect was that over a million recipients of disability benefits were excluded by stricter enforcement of criteria for entitlements.

In the UK public utilities and other major state-owned companies were privatised – water, rail, gas, British Telecom, British Aerospace, Rolls-Royce, British Airways – altogether more than forty state-owned corporations. If long-term consequences are a guide to the wisdom of the policy, one notes that the result has been higher prices and poorer quality services in essential UK sectors: polluted water is one, water company money being diverted to (largely foreign) shareholders instead of invested in maintaining and improving infrastructure; rail services are another, with the slowest trains and highest (indeed sky-high) fares in Europe; energy a third, with exorbitantly high costs compared to other European economies facing the same energy-supply stresses.[5]

Back in 1980s America, at the same time as increasing the defence budget by thirty-five per cent – Reagan's 'peace through strength' initiative aimed at beating the Soviet Union by forcing its own defence spending to unsustainable levels – the government cut income and corporate taxes sharply, dropping the highest marginal rate from seventy to twenty-eight per cent, removed price controls on energy, opened more public land to oil exploration, and cut environmental programmes. Despite tighter control of money supply through interest rate rises in the early 1980s to control inflation, the policies generated a boom, but with almost all the benefit going to the rich; middle-class incomes remained the same as they had been in the previous period of stagflation, and the poverty rate rose.[6]

Cutting taxes required borrowing more for military expenditure and what was left of social spending, so the deficit and the national debt both grew, tripling over Reagan's period in office. Both have continued to balloon upwards ever since, as the political necessity of holding down taxes and the practical necessity of increasing government spending pulled ever further apart. China joining the World Trade Organization in 2001 added to the problem, because the leap in its market share of cheap goods widened the trade imbalance with the US, the latter paying China for its products with IOUs, which means that China's holdings of US debt ballooned likewise – at time of writing China holds more than $850 billion of US debt.[7]

When emergency situations arose in 2008 (the near-collapse of the financial markets) and 2020 (the Covid-19 pandemic) with governments intervening to protect their own and the global economy, the ever-widening inequality gap was exacerbated by the measures taken – fuel added to the fire – because the bail-outs in both cases went mostly to corporations and their investors; 'socialism for the rich' in the much-used phrase, leaving all others to the unforgiving action of markets, in particular the labour market. Starting with the reduction of already weak trade union power in the US – in the UK in the 1980s Margaret Thatcher had already 'tamed' the unions legislatively and through tough responses to strikes in industries hard hit by her government's policies, notably mining – the result has been the evolution of a 'gig' market for labour, creating a 'precariat' of part-time and zero-hour contract workers, with few if any employment protections.

A compelling analysis of how this happens is the practice of central banks printing money to pump into the economy – 'quantitative easing' is the term of art – giving banks funds to lend to corporations and investors, who borrow it to buy their own shares on the stock market, thus increasing their value. The increased share value does not proportionally reflect increased profits, but far exceeds it; this is how the winners in the Covid pandemic grew startlingly so much wealthier in asset terms.

The 2008 crash had much to do with deregulation of economies in the preceding decades. The culture in financial centres such as the City of London and Wall Street had run out of control. In the US the fraudster Bernie Madoff (one of the greatest in history, to the tune of nearly $70 billion) benefitted from deregulation, escaping the scrutiny of a budget-squeezed, understaffed and powers-restricted Securities and Exchange Commission for over a decade after the first red flags were raised.[8] It was the events of 2008 that unmasked him, but the response to those events – 'quantitative easing' to keep most banks afloat – served to boost the position of large institutions and wealthy individuals while many 'ordinary people' lost their homes and savings. The financial institutions' deliberate but irresponsible packaging and sale of toxic assets such as sub-prime mortgages – loans that borrowers had insufficient income to repay – make these 'ordinary people' just as much victims as those Madoff robbed – which means that the financial institutions were as great fraudsters as he. 'Quantitative easing' kept most of the financial institutions afloat; none of their senior personnel were punished but instead, in outcome, actually rewarded. And since then the expedient of printing money to meet threats to the economic system has become a matter of course – with the money continuing to go to those who already have much, as the pandemic situation shows.

From Super PACs down to Elon Musk's crude bribery of swing state voters in the 2024 US presidential election with his $1 million a day sweepstake and large donations to the Trump campaign, the influence of big money on US elections is well known. People do not disburse large sums without expecting a return.[9] In Musk's case the return was a desk in the White House itself, promoting the chaotic Trump agenda of dismantling the US governmental structure; and also, by no coincidence, an increase in lucrative government contracts for Musk's companies. Within a state, big business can and invariably does seek to influence political parties, governments and elections, the power of their money giving them a super-vote and a degree of influence no individual voter can hope to wield, other than in rare circumstances where an outcome depends on a few ballots. Coupled with the recent rapid change in the nature of the capitalist system itself – perhaps its displacement by a new form of capitalism, or its overthrow by something worse – powered by the new digital technologies, the prospects for controlling this trend, still less reversing it, diminish.[10] The money-subversion of democracy could be handled within a state by legislation; but when real power is exercised by huge multinational entities lying outwith the jurisdiction of any single government, the corruption of democracy is unrestrainable. And this, as transnational corporations have grown in power and wealth increasingly over the course of the decades since 1980 – indeed, since the Second World War – is the chief problem. Enforcing standards, labour rights, transparency, ethical behaviour towards stakeholders and compliance with environmental protections, becomes harder if not impossible. Given that the overriding aim of business is to make profits, the expectation that businesses will think that profitability depends on responsible behaviour in these respects, and will act accordingly – even less, by tempering profits in the interest of such responsibilities – is, in too many cases, optimistic.

A study done in 2011 by a group of Zurich-based analysts showed that eighty per cent of corporate wealth was held by 700 transnational companies, half of it by just 147 of them.[11] Two-thirds of the world's assets were owned by 400 companies, who between them controlled seventy-per cent of world trade. Concentration of big business into even bigger business is a trend that the logic of business itself promotes, and has continued since the year of the Zurich group's study; mergers and acquisitions happen whenever and wherever scale brings benefits, both in larger market share and in reduced management costs. In a world in which capital, technology and the division of labour is internationalised, in which capital flows and exchange have created an integrated or at least interdependent international marketplace, the influence of national governments over economic factors within their borders is vastly reduced. Given that concentrations of economic power lead to concentrations of political power, the effect is that the direct and indirect influence of a small number of people – the decision makers in transnational businesses – is exerted over billions of others.

And these decision makers are likely to have little stake in any one national jurisdiction; their wealth is sequestered in offshore tax havens, immunising them from the negative effects of revenue-stressed governments on the fabric of civic life – revenue-stressed because so much of the rewards of business are not shared redistributively through taxation within a society, but drained out of it by tax avoidance schemes – in effect robbing states of resources for public services and support systems. It was estimated in 2016 that as much as $36 trillion sits in tax havens, the share from low-income countries exceeding the amount of foreign development aid they receive, and representing hundreds of billions in lost national tax revenues.[12]

Social strife is a ready outcome of gig work and economic insecurity, in the guise of low-wage 'labour flexibility', in circumstances of extremes of wealth inequality. In situations where some live in conspicuous luxury while others sleep on the street in all weathers, where trades unions have little bargaining power, where protest over environmental harms and against regimes which suppress minorities or wage war on weaker entities has little effect, discontent and turbulence are inevitable. If problems mount, it is not the vulnerable who are protected, but the interests of big business. The latter is comfortable with children working down mines or in sweatshops in the global South, with the continuance of discrimination against women and minorities, with poverty, homelessness, food insecurity and lack of healthcare at the bottom end of the economic scale everywhere. And this is to say nothing yet of the environmental damage caused by processes of extraction of natural resources and large-scale production and transportation of goods.[13]

The consumerism actively fostered by business has multiple negative effects. Not only does it impact the quality of individual and civic life by its focus on possession of often unnecessary goods as sources of satisfaction and status, but it operates as a major pull factor in economic migration of people from poorer to richer countries, and all this while harming the environment and climate. For just one striking example: areas of the Amazon rainforest ten times the size of Cornwall are annually cleared for cattle ranching to supply beef for beefburgers consumed in the US and elsewhere.[14]

Because transnational business influences governments but is not much influenced by them in return, and because it deprives states of revenue in the way described (its lobbying activities and payments to political parties are regarded as a very small cost of business), it is regarded with hostility by many. As John Kay points out, people 'hate the producers but love their products', thinking of Amazon, Apple and others.[15] But the chief effect is that transnational business's disempowerment of national government makes people angry about government policy, irrespective of whether they know the reason for the government's inability to serve their interests or answer their needs; and that infects attitudes to how governments are formed – in democracies, the democratic process itself. It is generally only in democracies that such discontent can be voiced without suppression in response, which, paradoxically, is an exacerbating factor, because the more ineffective protest proves, the greater the discontent grows.

What happens within a national economy is a symptom of the larger disease. To take a parochial example – exemplifying the macrocosm in the microcosm – consider the first Budget of the Labour Party government that came to power in the UK in 2024. Because of the chaos of the preceding Conservative Party government years, the effects of Covid stresses on the economy, and above all the strange reversal of Labour Party policy on Europe – its refusal to rejoin the European Single Market, Brexit having caused a massive hit to the national finances – the new government had to raise taxes. One proposal was to lift the maximum rate of tax on profits ('carried interest') from mergers and acquisitions activity from twenty-eight to forty-five per cent. Vigorous lobbying resulted in the government compromising at thirty-two per cent. According to the *Guardian* newspaper, fund managers were joyous (suffering, if that is the word, 'hangovers' after celebratory parties), one telling the paper that 'We got them down to 32% and made them feel like they had to be grateful for it'.[16] A statement from Tax Justice UK said:

This is a rare, in-plain-sight example of the super rich lobbying the government. Mostly this happens behind the scenes – but it is constant. This is what we're up against: powerful vested interests consistently lobbying the government to protect [their] interests ... We want to see a fairer tax system that takes more from the super-rich and wealthy companies to fund better public services: high quality healthcare, education, transport and social care. The vested interests want to see their power and wealth unchecked.[17]

A yet more striking example is the impact of Donald Trump's 2024 election victory. Even as results were coming in on election night, the New York Stock Exchange saw a big rise in stock values, and the chief gainers were the world's ten richest individuals, who collectively saw their wealth jump by $64 billion according to Bloomberg's 'Billionaire Index'.[18] CNN reported on the day after the election that:

> The biggest gainer was Elon Musk, the world's richest person and one of Trump's most outspoken and dedicated supporters, whose wealth jumped $26.5 billion to $290 billion Wednesday ... Amazon founder Jeff Bezos' wealth grew $7.1 billion a week after defending his decision to withhold the *Washington Post*'s endorsement of Vice President Kamala Harris. Oracle cofounder Larry Ellison, another Trump supporter, saw his net worth rise $5.5 billion Wednesday.
>
> Other gainers include former Microsoft executives Bill Gates and Steve Ballmer, former Google executives Larry Page and Sergey Brin and Berkshire Hathaway CEO Warren Buffett ...

Bloomberg notes it's the 'biggest daily increase' of wealth it's seen since the index began in 2012. The market rallied Wednesday as the election concluded swiftly and with expectations that Trump will usher in a new era of deregulation and other pro-business laws and policies investors believe could benefit the stock market overall – especially billionaires who hold much of the world's wealth.

'There is this huge perception of business friendly, tax-friendly regime coming into place, especially with them winning the Senate,' said Michael Block, chief operating officer at AgentSmyth.[19]

The connection between wealth accumulation among the few and right-wing politics is luminously demonstrated by this single event. However, the effect on stock values of Trump's volatile tariff policies after taking office in 2025 shows that once such politics has taken control, the unpredictability of the resulting administration can have significant downsides even for the wealthy.

The foregoing animadversions stand despite the fact, for fact it is, that transnational business has brought plenty of benefits too. The open international economic system it has forged and on which it relies has brought people and peoples together, fostered cultural exchange, encouraged innovations in technology, brought employment to many in developing economies, and lifted many millions out of poverty. It would be surprising, indeed incomprehensible, for transnational business to flourish if it had not brought benefits. But alas the benefits have been bought at great costs in the ways described. And if, as it threatens to do, it brings democracy down, and with it the rights, civil liberties and rule of law which are the principal goods of democracy, those benefits will be a very poor compensation.

In its Global Rights Index report issued in the late summer of 2024 the International Trade Union Confederation (ITUC), representing many among those who see the effects of globalised corporate power on individuals and societies close up, charged mega-businesses with 'financially supporting extremist political movements, fuelling climate crisis and violating labour and human rights'.[20] It identified corporations such as Amazon, Tesla, Meta, Blackstone and Vanguard as supporters of far-right political movements, their support aimed at protecting themselves from regulation and tax policies that would oblige them to conform to the same rates as smaller businesses. Evidence already mentioned is provided by Elon Musk's support of Donald Trump in the 2024 presidential election and Jeff Bezos, as owner of the *Washington Post*, refusing to allow his newspaper to endorse either of the candidates – a way of hedging bets and sending a silent message.[21]

The lobbying and financial backing of those who will serve mega-business interests extend beyond politicians to the United Nations and other international bodies. Mega-business wealth also buys a compliant, even sycophantic, media and (except in Russia and China) immunity from justice. According to the ITUC, this allows big transnational business to do what it specifically charges Amazon with: 'union busting and low wages on multiple continents, a monopoly in e-commerce, egregious carbon emissions through its Amazon Web Services data centers, corporate tax evasion and lobbying at national and international levels'. It goes on to accuse Amazon of poor workplace standards resulting in high injury rates among its more than a million workers worldwide, and notes that as the company was mounting a legal challenge over the constitutionality of the US National Labor Relations Board it was being banned by the European Parliament from lobbying activities, in reprisal for its refusal to discuss violations of labour rights.

The report's authors pointed to Tesla's opposition to trade unions in Germany and Sweden as well as the US, and Elon Musk's personal support for politicians and parties on the further right of the spectrum such as Trump, Javier Milei in Argentina, Narendra Modi in India, and the proto-Nazi AfD in Germany.[22] Meta invited criticism for giving its platforms to far-right movements, and lobbying to 'block legislation aimed at protecting citizens' private data'.[23] The value of such data to advertisers and political parties is great, and selling it is a source of revenue. The use made of 'big data' in political campaigns became controversial after exposés of the activities of Cambridge Analytica in 2016 influencing the UK's Brexit referendum.[24] The ITUC's report criticises ExxonMobil, Vanguard, Blackstone and Glencore for financing campaigns against environmental organisations and indigenous activists, citing ExxonMobil as an example of mega-business in the fossil fuel sector devoting efforts to undermining climate science or distracting from the energy sector's impact on global warming.[25]

The ITUC campaigns for an international treaty that will bind transnational business to human rights law. The case for saying that full observance of human rights provisions would solve many problems faced by individuals around the world seems idealistic but is a compelling one, as I have argued in *Discriminations*.[26]

If the fact that these ITUC labour-defending views invite a 'well they would say that, wouldn't they' response, a counterbalance is provided by the non-partisan US think tank Freedom House, which argues that democratic decline threatens business, and that protection of democracy's chief benefits – the rule of law, individual and group rights and freedoms – is essential to business.[27] In dispensations where these values are upheld the business environment is one of stability and predictability, both essential to making good decisions because the risk and opportunity factors required for due diligence assessments are clearer in an environment of steady, transparent and law-abiding government. In authoritarian outlooks supported by Musk and others, and in the view of those who think big profits are to be had in situations of chaos and disorder (a view propounded by Jacob Rees-Mogg's father William Rees-Mogg in *The Sovereign Individual*),[28] arbitrary decisions and switches of policy, corruption, the absence of checks and balances, the unreliability of information and the increased possibility of unrest, not only makes rational decision making difficult but increases the reluctance of investors both within and outside the polity.

Freedom House publishes an annual 'Freedom in the World Index', in 2024 providing dismaying evidence of decline in democracy and human rights since the first decade of the twenty-first century.[29] Its indices reveal that over three-quarters of the world's population live in countries where freedom is declining, including the US and UK. In the US Trump's attacks on the press and the claimed unreliability of electoral processes, in the UK clampdowns on the rights of assembly and protest, are troubling symptoms.[30]

Leaving aside the obvious cases of Russia, China and North Korea, matters are considerably worse elsewhere. Viktor Orbán's far-right government in Hungary changed election rules to benefit itself, attacked LGBTQ rights, imposed controls on teachers and judges, and introduced draconian provisions to keep out migrants.[31] The Hindu nationalist government of Narendra Modi in India mounted a major assault on human rights and the rule of law; according to the Amnesty International country report of 2023:

> National financial and investigation agencies were weaponized against civil society, human rights defenders, activists, journalists and critics, further shrinking civic space. Government officials, political leaders, and supporters of the Bharatiya Janata Party (BJP) ... advocated hatred and violence against religious minorities with impunity, particularly Muslims, marking a rise in hate crimes. Punitive demolitions of largely Muslim properties – including homes, businesses and places of worship – resulting in mass forced evictions after episodes of communal violence, were commonplace and went unpunished. India continued to impose arbitrary and blanket internet restrictions including internet shutdowns.[32]

In Myanmar (Burma) following another military coup in 2021 there was a continuing 'nationwide crackdown on millions of people opposed to its rule. The junta security forces have carried out mass killings, arbitrary arrests, torture, sexual violence, and other abuses that amount to crimes against humanity. Freedom of speech and assembly face severe restrictions.'[33] In Gaza the overwhelming ferocity of Israel's response to the atrocities committed in Hamas's incursion of 7 October 2023 exceeded what one would expect from a far-right Netanyahu government in the fraught conditions of that region. Despite Hamas's use of its own population as human shields, the total abandonment of the principle of proportionality in humanitarian laws of war was, to put the matter at a minimum, egregious.[34]

Some might think that business opportunities under an authoritarian regime are good because, if the regime is on one's side, it will facilitate one's activities and, with weak or non-existent regulation of standards and labour, costs will be lower. But the arbitrariness factor makes this a chancy matter.[35] In countries where democratic principles are upheld and relatively good governance prevails, there is a general culture of integrity, and business thrives on it, including the certainty it provides; trust can be placed in contracts and the security of patents. Where governments are suborned by business seeking to enhance its interests, their capture is a mark of weakness in the system, diminishing the longer-term prospect of matters ending well. Therefore, in their own best interests, Freedom House argues, business would be wise to promote democratic and human rights agendas. That means there is, in fact, a convergence between this perspective and the aims of the ITUC, when one takes an overall view.

The technological revolution of the decades preceding this writing has thrown these matters into sharper relief. Not only is the digital universe a site of opportunity for disrupters, propagandists, disseminators of misinformation and destabilisation – all this despite the positives that can be named also – but the effect on the global business environment itself has changed that environment in negative ways.

Economist Mordecai Kurz of Stanford University outlines the process in an article entitled 'How Capitalism Became a Threat to Democracy'.[36] The reason lies in the achievement of market dominance by innovating technology companies, the product of a 'winner takes all' situation in which victors in technology races first consolidate their position by blocking market entry with patents, and by acquiring rivals who see that joining them is more advantageous than competing with them. Deregulation has encouraged the growth of these monopolies, reprising the situation in the 'Gilded Age' of American capitalism in the half-century before the First World War. 'As a result, market power becomes a permanent feature of a capitalist economy. Technological competition is ineffective, and creative destruction does not restore economic efficiency … it also produces a concentration of economic and political power that threatens democracy, whose survival then becomes dependent on the creation of new policy tools to protect it.'[37]

Monopoly wealth, which is the value placed by stock markets on future monopoly profits, is distinct from capital income and material assets. By 2019 three-quarters of stock value on US markets consisted in monopoly wealth, with trading in it their chief activity. Because successful innovations sharply increase the value of technology stocks, and because the number of beneficiaries of this success is small – the innovators, early investors and financial advisors – large amounts of wealth quickly accumulate in very few hands. This explains the rapid increase in the number of US billionaires; by 2024 there were 756 of them.

'These economic and market dynamics', Kurz writes:

> have far-reaching political implications. One is high inequality, which is a direct result of a high degree of market power ... economic inequality creates political inequality, by giving the wealthy a stronger voice ... The main winners from free-market policy and rising market power since the 1980s have been the few in the top income stratum and the technically skilled with a college education, while unskilled workers without a college education have been most harmed ... Those who lost their livelihoods recognize that they are the victims of a policy choice. They paid the price for others to benefit, and for some to grow immensely wealthy, and American democracy has been weakened as a result. The evidence shows that most of the participants in the 6 January 2021 attack on the Capitol were former thriving workers who had been left behind.[38]

Kurz identifies 'a dangerous trifecta': rising market power, automation and globalisation. The first two have caused a decline in wages and rising inequality, the third has introduced challenges of the kind exemplified by China's economic surge and its detrimental effect on US manufacturing jobs.

HIGH FINANCE AND DEMOCRACY

When incomes fall the effects are social and regional – families and communities suffer from the retrenchment, and areas of the US associated with particular sectors (mining, steel, automobiles) experience an 'economic death'. Destabilisation follows in the form of resentment at governments perceived at being insensitive to the sufferers' plight, and hostility towards immigrants perceived as taking jobs or burdening support services. The victims of the trifecta's effects have accordingly, says Kurz, turned away from conventional politics and 'found a home in new anti-democratic movements such as Donald Trump's MAGA'.[39]

There is a paradox at work here – and if it is not a paradox it is a mark of something worse, which, as someone allergic to conspiracy theories, this writer would wish not to believe: but see the remarks below on 'movement conservatism' and the radicalisation of the US Republican Party. It is this: that the nexus between big money and right-wing politics is more than a natural socio-economic phenomenon, but a deliberately planned one. The influence of the beneficiaries of what Kurz calls the 'techno-winner-takes-all economy' – big companies and a handful of ultra-wealthy individuals – over politics and governments, steering them in rightward directions aimed at protecting and advantaging their interests, is too pat to be adventitious. The Supreme Court 'Citizens United' decision of 2010 which lifted restrictions on the use of corporate wealth for political purposes has proved to be an invaluable gift to them: the Super PAC phenomenon. The self-interests they thereby promote hurt those disadvantaged by them, yet these latter support the right-wing populist politicians whom the wealthy support, induced to believe that these politicians are on their side.

The outcries of the disaffected are potentiated by the use of social media, among the results a familiar litany of ill effects – mob behaviour, fake news, conspiracy theories and hate speech – all, as Kurz points out, protected by §230 of the US's somewhat misnamed Communications Decency Act of 1996, and much of it serving to promote division. Ultra-wealthy owners of social media platforms profit from this activity, using their profits to entrench the system harming those suffering under it. If this were indeed a deliberate strategy, it would be cynical in the extreme; if on the other hand the 'tech bros' are unwittingly sowing seeds of socio-economic disruptions that might eventually come to disadvantage them, it would be equally remarkable, this time for – at very least – its short-sightedness.

What those who vote for populist politicians want is what the latter tell them would solve their problems: jobs and an end to immigration, perhaps together with, in some way, punishing the 'elites' who have caused their misery. Since the real elites – the money elites – are supporters of the populist politicians, they jointly have to direct the ire of the disaffected away from themselves and point it elsewhere – to a different 'elite' consisting of the political opposition, 'liberals' and 'the woke' with their agendas on discrimination. Immigration is a particularly useful target, because inflaming hostility towards anyone regarded as foreign wishing to enter (and even those who have already entered) the country – economic migrants and asylum seekers are often lumped together – and introducing measures to deal with them, is a ready resource.

But the jobs question is more difficult, unless such measures as greening the economy are abandoned or reduced, or taxes are either raised to invest in job-creation conditions or lowered to incentivise entrepreneurial job-creators: both measures have their proponents among economic theorists. Raising taxes is always unpopular; keeping them down (the winning preference of wealthy supporters) makes it more difficult to pay for major campaigns to upskill workers, subsidise new industries that will provide secure well-paying jobs, and maintain social welfare programmes. (One measure promised by Donald Trump – protectionism, imposing high tariffs on foreign goods to promote domestic production and to repatriate production that had gone abroad in search of cheaper labour and fewer regulations – does not worry the new techno-elite; their wealth does not depend on ports, ships, trade agreements, export licences, and the rest, for they exist literally off the earth in the Cloud, operating without boundaries.)

Populist politicians thus ride to victory on the tiger's back, and then find themselves with a problem. Bridging the gap between promises and results is harder for them than for more 'small-c' conservative, normativity-observant politicians. In the past, populist governments have dealt with their problem by resort to undermining government and civil society structures and increasing distraction activities even, in some cases, to the extreme of engaging in external war. Being able to nominate and accuse alleged enemies, within or without the state, provides a prime distraction from a populist government's failures. As political scientist Michael W. Bauer put it:

> Populist governments pose a threat to liberal democracy by fostering a leadership cult, undermining minority rights, and disregarding norms of self-restraint ... Perhaps the most worrisome scenario is that of populists engaging in state transformation from the top position as heads of state or government. Once liberal democratic structures, procedures, and core state institutions are undermined, it can be difficult for a state to simply bounce back to the previous status quo. In fact, the state fabric may remain seriously de-pluralised in a populist manner.[40]

The situation of people in developing economies where transnational businesses operate is arguably worse, because the powerful influence exerted by international business on their governments makes countervailing efforts difficult. Such people therefore direct their resentment towards their own governments instead, which find themselves caught between a rock and a hard place, and the likelihood of their responding by oppression of their own people is all too great.

Whichever way one looks at it, the effect of very large business on economies and societies does not make a happy picture, not least in the impact on democracy. The argument put by Freedom House that business should actively promote democracy and human rights in its own interest is cogent, its several aspects hard to gainsay; yet the imperatives of the bottom line – profit – and the nature of the economy in the new age of digital technology both militate against it. The kinds of businesses that produce tangible goods and services have not internationalised out of charity, but because labour costs and the costs of meeting regulatory standards are lower in cheap-labour countries. The new mega-sized techno-businesses have reshaped markets, not least stock markets, and through monopoly power have turned them into milch cows, increasing their wealth by tens of millions of dollars a day. Stock markets are in large part disconnected from the ground-level realities in an economy. With the influence thus accrued, big companies and wealthy individuals come to have a vote equal to millions of other people's votes: and that is not democracy.

The logic of big business's capture of government is that it would like government to get out of the way, literally. And this has been happening to an increasing extent since the late 1950s in the form of Special Economic Zones (SEZs). These are parts of a country where regulations are different from elsewhere in the country in order to be more favourable to business, especially in tax terms. The aim is to encourage investment, especially foreign direct investment. China is the most successful example of an economy making use of SEZs.

SEZs take a number of forms: Free Trade Zones, Export Processing Zones, Industrial Parks and Special Zones. Free Trade Zones and Export Processing Zones are enclosed areas in which imports and exports are processed with special, often duty-free, customs procedures; they are extensions of the bonded warehouse concept. As the name implies, Industrial Parks are areas specific to industrial (thus not commercial or residential) activity favoured by tax-related incentives. Special Zones include technology and logistics hubs and airport areas. Extension of the idea to agricultural zones, and to business areas in cities, is a natural corollary.

China's SEZs, set up to attract foreign capital, have been notably successful. Initially five were created – in 1983, Shenzhen, Zhuhai and Shantou in Guangdong province and Xiamen in Fujian province, soon followed in 1984 by Hainan Island. Since then a further fourteen coastal 'open cities' have been designated. They offer significant incentives to foreign investors, among other things permitting tax-free import of technology and equipment.

The liberties enjoyed by SEZs are not restricted to tax and duty incentives only. They extend to exemption from laws on employment, planning and property, and this in turn involves the disapplication of some of the state's legal and judicial framework.

The success in economic terms of the model has prompted enthusiasm for them in the UK. Policy for the creation of SEZs was introduced in 2011. During the short-lived premiership of Liz Truss in 2022 all local authorities were encouraged to apply to become SEZs, saying that not just business but personal taxes could be slashed within them. Despite Truss's fall SEZs remained government policy, and many local councils, suffering severe financial distress (largely because of government cuts), were attracted by the idea of private enterprise taking over some or even many of their functions. To critics, this was just one more example of public services being privatised, and public money being transferred to private hands. An example cited by critics is the Teesside Freeport project; they say that public land was sold to a group formed by the town's mayor at £1 an acre, and that after public money was used to clear the land its value increased many times over, £50 million in profits being distributed to the shareholders in the first year of operation.[41]

At time of writing there are forty-eight SEZs in the UK. The UK government website 'Guidance on Enterprise Zones' announces business rate discounts of up to 100 per cent over five years, enhanced Capital Allowances for machinery and equipment, and simplified planning regulations. Because growth in business rates is retained by the local authority, and because employment opportunities in the zones are increased, the principle of the project looks good. But concerns about them multiply. An example is the Plymouth and South Devon Freeport SEZ. There was no public consultation on its introduction, and subsequent citizen worries about the fact that the zone extends so far that it includes the whole of Dartmoor, a large area of hitherto protected natural beauty, was met with silence from the local authority, or refusals to respond to information requests on the grounds of 'commercial sensitivity'.[42]

The Plymouth and South Devon situation is not unique. The boundaries of some of the SEZs include other protected nature reserves, national parks, the North Yorkshire Moors, the New Forest, the entire Isle of Wight, and the designated 'Area of Outstanding Natural Beauty' of the Suffolk Coast and Heaths conservation region.

SEZs are private enterprise tax-break zones. They are proliferating in developing economies in East Africa, South-East

Asia and the Arabian peninsula where their 'negative impacts including ecological disasters, little respect for human rights, no accountability to any public, and unprecedented corruption' illustrate the dangers implicit.[43] The logical terminus of SEZs is the privately owned autonomous city-state or 'charter city', of which a major example is Próspera off the coast of Honduras. The concept of these is 'particularly attractive to a brand of right-wing libertarian thinking which is globally represented by an affiliated group of powerful think tanks', significantly named the 'Atlas Network' (Ayn Rand's 1957 novel *Atlas Shrugged* is the point of reference).[44] This organisation is the 'brainchild of the founder of the Institute of Economic Affairs (IEA) and former battery-chicken farmer, Antony Fisher'. It operates by incorporating:

> many familiar 'institutes', 'research groups' and 'foundations', most claiming charitable status, which renders the convenient advantage of donor anonymity. Several leaks and investigations have nonetheless managed to trace significant funding back to American libertarian billionaires and top players in industries whose activities have been restricted by government regulation, for example fossil fuels, tobacco, and gambling. Globally, there are between 450 and 500 think tanks in the Atlas Network.[45]

The Atlas Network enjoys direct and influential access to political parties and government. In the UK case this is:

> well illustrated by the presence of two influential Atlas advocates and charter city enthusiasts, Shanker Singham and Peter

Thiel. Singham was formerly economics director at the Legatum Institute, before leaving to head up a trade unit at the IEA, and was accorded unparalleled access to senior British politicians during the Brexit negotiations, much to the bafflement of other negotiators present, and one of his main policy objectives was the creation of 'prosperity zones'.[46]

Singham served as a 'special advisor to Liz Truss before and during her brief tenure in Downing Street and was co-chair of her Growth Commission. He also led the successful bids for the new Welsh freeports.'[47] Facebook investor, PayPal co-founder and Palantir Technologies founder Peter Thiel (at a net worth of $11 billion he is 'only' 212th on the Bloomberg Billionaires Index as of July 2024) is an exemplary poster boy for the libertarian right; the Wikipedia entry on him is scripture for this outlook and merits a read, though not for the faint-hearted.[48] Even before Palantir won the UK's health service data contract, a deal worth £330 million, Thiel said that the NHS should be 'ripped up to start over' in private ownership.[49]

The most salient recent example of Atlas thinking is the aforementioned charter city Próspera LLC on the Honduran island of Roatán. Thiel is one of the owners; Singham is an advisor to it. Próspera's website announces it as 'a startup city with a regulatory system designed for entrepreneurs to build better, cheaper, and faster than anywhere else in the world.'[50] It is the brainchild of the American libertarian economist Paul Romer (the professor who taught former British Prime Minister Rishi Sunak at Stanford University). Its legal and regulatory regimes are independent of Honduras – it has its own judicial, economic and administrative system – and the company that manages it, Honduras Próspera Inc., owned by Pronomos Capital, has a veto vote in Roatán's governing council. Honduras's laws creating Zones of Employment and Economic Development made it possible for Pronomos to set Próspera up when Juan Orlando Hernández was President of Honduras, but following his departure (facing unrelated felony charges) the successor government declared it unconstitutional. In response Próspera's owners sued the Honduran government for $11 billion, the sum they claim to have lost in profits; this figure is two-thirds of the Honduran annual budget.[51]

As the logical terminus of libertarian economic thinking – the wholly privatised company-run for-profit state – Próspera demonstrates, among other things, the remarkable influence of Ayn Rand. In her novel *Atlas Shrugged* she depicts the US in an unspecified dystopian future with the economy approaching collapse and business decisions being made unwisely, corruptly, and with overweening government interference. Mysterious references to someone called John Galt eventually lead to the discovery that the individual so named has led business leaders on a 'strike' in protest at the economic arrangements responsible for the chaos; they have accompanied him to 'Galt's Gulch' and there hidden from the world. Persuaded by his lover to leave his hideaway, Galt goes to New York and delivers a three-hour lecture over public radio outlining Ayn Rand's philosophy ('Objectivism', promoting 'rational selfishness' and the right to property). He castigates the practice of government taking the rewards of entrepreneurship from productive people to redistribute it through taxation to 'parasites and moochers', describing government bureaucrats as 'looters'. The novel was on the bestseller list for twenty-two weeks after publication, and has since sold more than ten million copies.[52]

Alan Greenspan, first appointed to the US Federal Reserve by Ronald Reagan and chairman of it for twenty years, was a friend and admirer of Rand, and a member of her inner circle; before his official career he gave lectures on her economic theories and those of his other influences, Milton Friedman and Friedrich Hayek.[53] The fact that the US put only a watered-down version of these ideas into practice, significant though their application was, has encouraged the view among some that to get them implemented properly requires a bold destruction and then reconstruction of the existing economic order. This theory is known as 'accelerationism'. An example of it in practice at a smaller scale is preparation of the UK's National Health System for privatisation by underfunding it to the extent of collapse – some claim that creeping privatisation has being going on for several decades[54] – while at the larger scale the aim is collapsing the whole economy so that it can be restructured from the ground up.[55]

Accelerationism has long had proponents on both the further left and further right of politics, agreeing with each other in one, but major, respect: that by pushing contemporary capitalism to its limits it will self-destruct, clearing the way for their respective versions of utopia to follow. The left version has all but faded from the picture; it is the right version that increasingly attracts. SEZs and Próspera-style enclaves are promissory notes for the profit-making utopia it portrays. For libertarian economists the factors that inhibit wealth creation are the laws, regulatory structures and taxes that exist for the wide palette of state and social concerns that government addresses. To get them out of the way, government has to be reduced to a minimum, or – as in Próspera – privatised wholly. This would mean that health, education, security, infrastructure, environmental and consumer protections, planning, safety standards for medicines, food, buildings, machinery and electrical equipment, licensing of professional practitioners of all kinds, and more, would be provided, if at all, by private enterprise. It is already the case that libertarians think health and education should not be regarded as publicly provided goods, but instead that there should be a market in them; this is partially the case anyway, higher quality versions of them being available for purchase almost everywhere. For an example of what a post-accelerated world would be like, there would not be a public fire brigade, but individuals would subscribe to a private fire brigade service – if they can afford it among the many other calls on their purses for the other things that communal provision through taxation once supplied.

It is already the case that poverty is a political choice. In a Próspera-style future there would not merely be less but no safety-net for those without the talent to compete in a raw market. This does not trouble economic libertarians, who from Andrew Carnegie in the nineteenth century to Elon Musk today have anyway regarded success in the accumulation of individual wealth as the mark of superior people – to the extent of the latter promoting a form of eugenics in which wealthy people have as many children as they can (he has at least twelve), an implication of 'pronatalism' being that unsuccessful people should have none. A Bloomberg article reports that:

> Musk has become the richest and most powerful person who's loudly of like mind with the pronatalist movement, a loose confederation of religious conservatives, libertarian techies and blogger bros. Most pro-natalists say their priorities centre around incentivizing parenthood economically and politically. In practice, some leading pro-natalists oppose abortion and birth control, too, and have been known to fret about declines in the proportion of White Americans and advocate for the forcible reversal of that trend. 'The pronatalist and the eugenic positions are very much not in opposition', Kevin Dolan, the organiser of a pronatalist conference, said on a podcast last year. 'They're very much aligned.'[56]

In discussing Musk's support for the Population Wellbeing Initiative at the University of Texas at Austin, Techcrunch.com stated that Musk's 'pronatalism, reportedly, was borne out a desire to prevent the demise of what Musk considers "advanced society" through the declining fertility of the intellectually gifted. *Business Insider* has reported previously that Musk believes that wealth is directly linked to IQ and has urged "all the rich men he knew" to have as many children as possible.'[57]

The various side-interests of economic libertarians might look like a form of play; plenty of people have nonconformist ideas but, unlike major celebrities, the furthest they can propagate them is to a silo of followers on a social media platform if they have one. But one has to ask, in thinking of what the world would look like if it becomes Próspera, whether such ideas might be put into effect. It has happened before; the history of eugenics is a chillingly educative one.[58] Proponents of the Próspera ideal, opposed to control by government regulators and taxers, would have to control the labourers who sweep the streets, carry the boxes, empty the bins, replace the light bulbs, cook the dinners and wash the dishes afterwards; and that could extend to whether they have children, given the social views that accompany their economic ones. It seems unthinkable, but from Plato's *Republic* to Nazi Germany the same idea has been in play, and has actually been put into practice in recent history, not just in Nazi Germany but in the US itself: in thirty-two states federally-funded forced sterilisation of 'undesirables' occurred in the early part of the twentieth century.[59]

> In 1927, the U.S. Supreme Court decided, by a vote of 8 to 1, to uphold a state's right to forcibly sterilise a person considered unfit to procreate. The case, known as *Buck v. Bell*, centred on a young woman named Carrie Buck, whom the state of Virginia had deemed to be 'feebleminded.' [It] was considered a victory for America's eugenics movement, an early twentieth-century school of thought that emphasized biological determinism and actively sought to 'breed out' traits that were considered undesirable.[60]

HIGH FINANCE AND DEMOCRACY

Seven thousand cases of forced sterilization followed *Buck v. Bell*.[61]

These points are made to emphasise that economic libertarianism does not stop at economics, but impacts society widely, and could reach these extremes if their logic is followed to the limit. The world is moving in that direction, more rapidly than is comfortable. The apparently unassailable piety that growth is everything, that profits matter so much that other considerations can be swept from its path, that wealth is such a good in itself that unlimited amounts of it are still better, leads to the practical and successful effort by proponents of these ideas to fashion politics and society in such a way that the ideas turn into practical realities. They do so already in ways that damage individual lives and undermine democracy with its constituent apparatus of the rule of law, rights and liberties – these latter increasingly becoming the purchased possession of very few. The idea that economic growth and the pursuit of profit should be tempered in the interests of individual well-being and less unequal societies is anathema to those in the vanguard of economic libertarianism. Democracy, especially if properly implemented, stands in their way.

People at the tough end of these developments probably do not think much about such seeming-abstractions as the rule of law and human rights. Facing unemployment, or working two jobs to make ends meet, they do not blame the entities that are actually immiserating them; they blame the system as it appears to them *prima facie*. The system is democracy, the governments it produces are weak because suborned by powerful transnational businesses and mega-rich individuals, but the people do not see that side of the equation, they only see the ineffectiveness of the system and the way it has left them behind.[62] The attraction of populist alternatives is explained by this, but the tragedy lies in the fact that populism, once it has used the democratic licence of support for it as the promise-making alternative, has a tendency to employ it as a licence to end democracy and its precious – but to the populist politicians and their backers, obstructive – rule of law, rights and freedoms. Hitler, remember, was democratically elected in the last election to be held until after his death.

The story told here of the rise of big money's influence on politics, especially in the US, requires the closely connected story of the rightward radicalisation of the Republican Party from the Reagan era onwards. It was then, and at time of writing remains, a conscious programme that goes under the name of 'movement conservatism'. Donald Trump is the outcome of the process it initiated, putting into practice techniques of disruption and distraction in order to dismantle the US polity which it sees as root and branch infected by liberalism. Trump's initiatives as his second presidential term began in 2025 is exactly what the 'movement conservatism' agenda aims at. How far the political spectrum has been shifted by it is illustrated by the fact that the *New York Times* published an interview with one Curtis Yarvin, a formerly obscure blogger of extremist views, or what would once have been considered such, until the *New York Times* and others took an interest in him and thereby endowed him with a degree of credibility. Yarvin, the newspaper reports, says that '"democracy is done" and argues that government bureaucracy should be radically gutted, and perhaps most provocative, he argues that American democracy should be replaced by what he calls a "monarchy" run by what he has called a "C.E.O." – basically his friendlier term for a dictator.'[63]

'Movement conservatism' first began to intensify its opposition in response to the liberalising of US society in the 1960s and 70s – the Civil Rights movement, 'second wave' feminism, gay rights, *Roe v. Wade*. It found a ready ally in the 'religious right' then becoming politically organised, and the alliance increased in influence over the following decades, gaining for itself more seats in Congress and a more assertive media presence. Newt Gingrich was a leading figure in this by the 1990s.[64]

> Movement conservatives had a vanguardist mentality – they were insurrectionists assaulting the liberal establishment's castle. Newt Gingrich embodied and advanced this outlook more than anyone. The outlook set in train a dynamic that still holds true today: Conservatives are disruptors who constantly question the status quo; liberals are defenders of the existing order.[65]

The combined and mutually reinforcing alliance of big money and radical conservatism has, at time of writing, won the day in the US in the figure of Trump. Despite reservations one might have about conspiracy theories, failure to recognise that both the 'movement conservative' programme and its proponents have been engaged in exerting themselves in other countries is a mistake. Steve Bannon's open intervention in European politics through his Brussels-based organisation actually called 'The Movement' is a case in point; see below.

It is not possible to discuss the effect of international business without, finally, mentioning one of its worst manifestations: the arms trade and the conflicts on which its vast profits depend. The effects on people and planet of the matters already discussed are bad enough, but the arms trade adds a whole further dimension. Moreover it happens with far too little public discussion, despite the enormities involved.

Entities involved in the manufacture, trade, and research and development of weapons and associated systems collectively go by the name 'the defence industry', the word 'defence' providing a positive gloss. Certainly, in a world occupied by a still-infantile humanity ready to use violence to solve problems or make gains, defence capability is a necessity. It is a natural corollary that countries which produce armaments and train militaries should wish allies to be prepared for conflict also, and to sell them some of its defence products.

But the 'defence industry' is not restricted to the benign endeavour of protecting one's own. In an unstable world there are plenty of buyers, and therefore large profits to be made – the more conflicts, the larger the profits. It verges on conspiracy theory to suggest that deliberate fomentation of conflict is a strategy of some producers, for conditions in too many places are fomenting enough by themselves. But the question whether there is responsible governance in the arms business regarding who buys weapons, of what kind and for what purposes, presses; do arms traders ask these questions, and answer them morally? Do governments ensure that public and private developers, producers and marketers of arms do so? Almost certainly not, apart from fig-leaf pronouncements to the contrary. As openDemocracy puts it, 'Our global culture of war means guaranteed profits for the arms industry'; for the industry 'to flourish, it needs wars, preferably protracted, [and] destructive stalemates in far-off places ... For arms dealers, a "perfect war" is one that degenerates into a violent stalemate that creates an insatiable demand for arms.'[66]

The principal monitor of the global arms trade is the Stockholm International Peace Research Institute (SIPRI), from whose published databases the following is quoted.[67] According to SIPRI, the largest producers and exporters of arms are the US, France, Russia, China and Germany in that order, between them supplying three-quarters of the world's arms and weapons systems. Globally, expenditure on armaments reached nearly $2.5 trillion in 2024, having risen steeply over the previous fifteen years to levels previously only experienced at the tensest periods of the Cold War. Most major armaments and associated defence technologies are bought by national militaries, deployed in conflicts such as the first and second Gulf wars, Afghanistan, Syria, the Russia–Ukraine war and the conflicts between Israel and its neighbours. But civil wars are fought largely with small arms, of which in 2024 over a billion were in circulation, eighty-five per cent of them in civilian hands.[68] 'Civilian hands' includes the ad hoc militias of excited young men brandishing Kalashnikovs as they career about in open trucks in strife-torn parts of Africa and Arabia.

An armaments company has a compelling case to make to government. First, continuous research and development is a necessity, to compete or ideally to get ahead of potential enemies in weapons effectiveness. History affirms the obvious fact that technologically superior weaponry is a principal factor in military success.[69] Second, to pay for the development and manufacture of weapons by selling some of them abroad is not merely a good but a guaranteed source of revenue, lightening the burden on government military expenditure. Third, a foreign ally dependent on one's own industry for installation, training, maintenance and resupply of weapons systems keeps that revenue flowing. Of course, allies might not be offered the very best or latest technology, for – who knows? – allies can become enemies, but they will buy what they are offered. The combined imperatives of security and profit in a turbulent world make these arguments irresistible.

By its very existence the arms industry normalises war, and renders acceptable to most people the idea that it is both legal and morally legitimate to devote enormous resources – resources that might otherwise be spent on education, health, good housing, protection of the environment, and more – to producing the means for killing people and destroying cities. Viewed in this light, the business of war is a manifestation of a sickness in humanity. It entails that major corporate enterprises are based upon – and for their continued success require – enmity between people and peoples: 'no business without enemies' as Jordi Calvo Rufanges put it.[70] Given that investment in the infrastructure of the arms trade is so great (research facilities, factories, employees, shipping, arms fairs, etc.), and the profits so large, drawing attention to the victims of war and the damage to physical and psychological social structures carries no weight. As with the ineffectiveness of ugly images on cigarette packs intended to stop people smoking, newsreel footage of corpses, maimed and blinded children, smoking ruins, traumatised citizenries, legless veterans, does not diminish the profits of the arms trade by a single dollar.

That is the power of international business: in too many cases not discouraged from making money out of bad things made worse by the very fact of making money out of them.[71] Even if business acknowledged that its negative pressure on democracy might harm itself in the longer term, the short-term advantages it harvests are too seductive to stop doing it.[72] As the foregoing argues, this is of a piece with the general suicidal tendencies of humanity: live now, pay later, the future must look after itself as best it can. Profit comes first, and democracy stands in its way.

3

THE ALTERNATIVE MODEL: TURNING TO AUTHORITARIANISM

In the six decades after the Second World War the number of democracies in the world more than quadrupled. Decolonisation in the period between the 1950s and 1970s, and then the fall of the Soviet Union between 1989 and 1991 – which saw the emergence of thirty newly independent states, seventeen of which adopted democratic constitutions – meant that by the second decade of the twenty-first century the number of recognised democracies around the world was at an all-time high: on one measure, ninety-seven out of 167 countries (fifty-eight per cent) were rated as democracies, only twenty-one (thirteen per cent) as autocracies, the rest not counting as democracies because they were either mixed or in a state of transition (twenty-six per cent), or omitted from the research because of conflict, foreign intervention or occupation – at the time of the survey in 2017 there were five such.[1]

THE ALTERNATIVE MODEL

But even as these figures were being published by the Pew Research Center, there had already begun a sharp decline in democratic indices and a correlative rise in authoritarianism. Among the states where indices declined – already apparent in the Pew data – were the US and the UK.[2] Since then matters have become worse. By 2021, the US had slid down the democracy index from ninety points to eighty-three, not just worse than the Western European democracies but worse even than relatively new democracies such as Argentina and Taiwan.[3]

The upward democratic turn began after 1945 as a conscious endeavour by the war's victors to establish a new basis for the reorganisation of the international community. The UN's Universal Declaration of Human Rights stated that 'The will of the people shall be the basis of the authority of the government ... expressed in periodic and genuine elections which shall be by universal suffrage and shall be held by secret vote or by equivalent free voting procedures.' Both the Organization of American States (OAS) and the Council of Europe affirmed the principle, the former stating at the outset its aim 'to promote and consolidate representative democracy'.[4]

The UN's Universal Declaration was just that, a *declaration*, not an international treaty; over the following two decades its principles were given fuller statement, and elevated into international law, by two International Covenants: on Civil and Political Rights and on Economic, Social and Cultural Rights. Introduction of the former, enshrining the democratic principle, was delayed by hesitancies on the part of the US and the Soviet Union because of

Cold War geopolitical considerations, but concerted efforts by newly independent former colonies pushed its adoption forward, and the Covenant was formally adopted in 1966 and came into international legal force ten years later.

A practical aspect of democratisation endeavours was the appointment of observers at elections. Although the UN did not officially accept invitations to send observers until 1990 (in Nicaragua), maintaining a general principle that it would do so only when self-determination in an until-then dependent territory was at issue, the practice itself began immediately, early examples being South Korea in 1948, Togoland in 1956 and 1958, and Costa Rica in 1962. In these cases observation was conducted by the US, the UK, France and the OAS, the latter thereafter undertaking numerous observation exercises in Central and South American member states.[5] Election observation became fully an international norm by the end of the twentieth century, to the extent that when in 2009 Iran refused to admit observers it was widely assumed that its elections that year were tainted.[6]

A significant feature of the OAS's observation programme was its stated aim of providing 'moral support for democratic elections', while a number of international NGOs used the opportunity to 'take advantage of the openness provided by an election to investigate specific cases involving allegations of human rights violations', a fact that some regimes used to claim interference and violation of sovereignty.[7]

But election observation was only one, and perhaps relatively minor, factor in the world's increasing democratisation after 1945. Much more impactful was the conjoining of aid

THE ALTERNATIVE MODEL

with the demand that recipient nations adopt democratic procedures. One example is President John F. Kennedy's 'Alliance for Progress' programme, which sent $22.3 billion (in value $229.7 billion at time of writing) to Latin America for this purpose. But in fact US foreign policy had a more pressing aim than promoting democracy, namely, stopping the spread of communism; a democratically elected communist government was not a candidate for aid dollars, as demonstrated by Argentina under Arturo Frondizi (President of Argentina 1958–1962; he was overthrown by a military coup) and the OAS's suspension of Cuban participation – at US insistence – three years after its 1959 revolution.[8]

In short, development aid was dependent on democracy producing outcomes that aligned with US interests. This has always mattered so much more than democracy itself that the US has frequently supported autocrats whenever convenient: in 2017 a *HuffPost* article reported that:

> Many of the 45 present-day undemocratic US base hosts qualify as fully 'authoritarian regimes,' according to the Economist Democracy Index.[9] In such cases, American installations and the troops stationed on them are effectively helping block the spread of democracy in countries like Cameroon, Chad, Ethiopia, Jordan, Kuwait, Niger, Oman, Qatar, Saudi Arabia, and the United Arab Emirates.[10]

If one is serious about democracy it cannot carry the proviso 'only if it produces the right result' according to a partisan view of what counts as 'right'. Yet in one respect the conditionality on aid had a point, because the phenomenon of a 'one last time' democratic vote, giving power to an authoritarian regime that thereafter dismantles democracy, is altogether too common; given the choice when other foreign policy objectives are unaffected by it, aid-giving countries prefer genuine democracies to autocracies for pragmatic reasons, and development aid – more precisely, the threat to suspend it – provides leverage against backsliding by populist leaders. Moreover, the UN Sustainable Development Group urged that conditionality should include a requirement to observe human rights norms, which, though by no means invariably successful, give at least some protection to minorities and some moral support to opposition groups in the countries in question.[11]

The conditionality of aid on democratisation and human rights norms was therefore a factor in democracy's continuing spread until the recent reversal. Allied to it was the perception that the power and economic success of the West owed itself to the system; North America, Western Europe and Australasia presented a model, so compelling that in India and elsewhere, when democracy faltered as under Indira Gandhi between 1975 and 1977, the outcry was premised on the model's unquestioned desirability. The contrast between East and West Germany before the fall of the Berlin Wall in 1989 was a vivid example of the contrast between democracy and its absence. Even the appropriation of 'democratic' as a feel-good term in the names of markedly undemocratic regimes – 'The German Democratic Republic' (East Germany) and 'The Democratic People's Republic of Korea' (North Korea) – illustrate this.

THE ALTERNATIVE MODEL

But now the trend to democratisation has reversed, and a significant feature of this reversal is that autocrats' methods for achieving power have latterly changed from coups and military take-overs to subtler strategies. They have learned how to counter the previous democratisation trend by exploiting aspects of it that serve them.[12] As Ruth Ben-Ghiat points out:

> Elections had long been a mark of an open society and their absence a criterion of autocracy, but new authoritarians use elections to keep themselves in office, deploying antidemocratic tactics like fraud or voter suppression to get the results they need. The resources they devote to rigging elections are often well spent. Leaders who come to power by elections rather than coups are more likely to avoid ejection from office and less likely to face punishment. Once a new authoritarian establishes control, he may stay in office as long as some old-school dictators. A 2020 amendment to the Russian constitution allows Putin, who has already been president for a total of sixteen years, to remain head of state until 2036.[13]

Among the factors that explain the dramatic reversal, these two are salient: first, the models offered by Singapore and most especially China as states surging in economic power while maintaining strict social and political control, the latter a major reason for the former; and second, the yeasting of right-wing movements within democracies themselves, allied in significant cases with high finance interests as outlined in the previous chapter and evidenced by, among many other sources, the 2023 report to the Committee on Political Affairs and Democracy of the European Parliament, titled 'The Challenge of Far-Right Ideology to Democracy and Human Rights in Europe'.[14]

Consider each of these factors in turn.

The Chinese model speaks for itself.[15] One has only to consider what political leaders contemplating it would see as its attractions; achievement of economic growth and international influence while staying permanently in power, as the Chinese Communist Party (CCP) has done since 1949. Add to this the vigorous extension of Chinese influence in the form of its dominating presence in a number of African countries, the dependence on trading relations with it of economies like Australia, and the sheer size of its presence in the Asia-Pacific region – and one sees that even if the Chinese model were not attractive enough by itself, its economic and geopolitical draw would be sufficient, as the US draw had been since 1945 and as was the British Empire's draw before that. China is the largest provider of development finance in the world, its 'Belt and Road Initiative' impacting 150 countries along the historic and new Silk Road routes; and it is not interested in democracy promotion – very much the opposite.[16]

The other factor, the far-right challenge discussed in the European Parliament report, is likewise in plain sight. One example, already mentioned, is 'The Movement' founded by Steve Bannon, officially registered and based in Brussels. It is explicit in its aims, which are identified as seeking to capture as many seats in the EU Parliament as possible in order to dismantle the EU itself,[17] and counteracting such movements as George Soros's 'Open Society Foundations' with their opposite aim of 'supporting civil society groups to build vibrant and inclusive democracies whose governments are accountable to their people' in order to promote justice, education and independent media.[18] Bannon and 'The Movement' might not be as significant in themselves as they would wish, despite the warmth initially extended to them by far-right parties in Hungary, Poland, Italy and the UK – several of which have since distanced themselves from Bannon, such as Marine Le Pen's Rassemblement National (National Rally) in France and the Alternative für Deutschland (AfD) in Germany – but the kind of ideas 'The Movement' promotes have gained not just traction but palpable influence more widely in Europe, and their success in the US makes their influence in Europe more rather than less likely.[19]

Far-right politics trade on nationalism and associated anti-immigration sentiment, with ideas of cultural identity, 'traditional' cultural norms and even ethnic 'purity' to the fore. These manifest as xenophobia, racism and (in line with traditionalist – which in practice means masculinist – sentiment) sexism. Disaffection on the part of those who feel themselves oppressed by economic circumstances responds readily to the claim that it is immigrants and (among men, especially younger men) the social and economic empowerment of women that are among the factors to blame. They see in 'wokeism' and growing ethnic diversity in their countries conspicuous signs of what they take to disadvantage them, and blame (are told by populist politicians to blame) 'liberal elites' for allowing this to happen. Populist politicians exploit and inflame these sentiments to gain power. Resulting authoritarian governments act on the sentiments they exploited to get into power by clamping down on immigration, reversing some of the gains of feminism (reintroduction of abortion bans is an example), and opposing gay rights, same-sex marriage and alternative lifestyles. These policies are meat tossed to the political base, but they are not the main reason why populist politicians seek power. The main reason is that democracy and its constituent features of free discussion, the achievement of consent, a law- and rules-based order, rights and entitlements, and critical scrutiny by a free press, are barriers to their getting and thereafter retaining power. Populism in politics leads directly to authoritarianism.

Centrist politics is not without blame for giving far-right politics its chance. In the decades before this writing, austerity measures and deficit control, the failure to tax big money adequately and to prevent the off-shoring of trillions in wealth, played a major part. These policy choices – encouraged by the high finance interests whom centrist politicians hoped would, by thus incentivising them, rescue their economies – have over the last few decades, and especially since 2008, degraded the civic fabric and left enough people struggling to provide populist politicians with fertile ground. Those policy choices have driven inequality, and inequality is toxic. It did not take long for populist politicians to exploit this toxicity by taking their chance – again: by blaming immigrants, liberal culture and the reigning socio-political establishment.

THE ALTERNATIVE MODEL

This has been a major failure of democratic leadership. True statesmen and -women are people who tirelessly explain, coax, take the right and honest tough choices irrespective of their own political careers. They have, and are meant to act upon, the responsibility to serve the people's interests – all the people: the '*of* the people' people. Populism replaces statesmen and -women with demagogues, who serve their own interests, the interests of the subsets consisting of the '*by* and *for*' people in an authoritarian state – namely, those who rule, those who benefit, but certainly not the majority, given that the majority consists of many minorities.

In Appendix I are two speculative examples of how matters might have worked out differently if statesmanship had been available in the US and UK in the second decade of the twenty-first century.

Authoritarianism takes different forms, but they all share a common feature: centralised control, the manipulation of institutions to preserve the government (or supreme individual) in power, and the reduction of civil liberties. The thread combining these features is the abandonment, outright or more subtly, of the rule of law; either the governing individual or group is above the law or overrides it at their convenience, or bends it to their purposes either by interference in legal processes or by changing the laws to suit themselves. Putin's rewriting of the Russian Federation's Constitution to keep himself in power, in effect permanently, is a classic case of the latter.

The differences between autocracy, totalitarianism and fascism are superficial. *Autocracy* or dictatorship is rule by a single unrestrained individual, undisguised as in absolute monarchy or disguised by the trappings of apparent party government over which one person is supreme. A *totalitarian* regime is one in which everyone in the state is subordinate to and conscripted by its commands, assigned to tasks and roles at the state's direction, coerced to obey if unwilling, and living under continual threat of that coercion and of punishment for failing to obey. *Fascism* is a nationalistic or ethnic ideology in which a centralised party or leader places an idealised State or Nation (which means, the governing power itself) above individuals, suppresses opposition and criticism, and regiments the society to serve its economic and often military aspirations.

How authoritarianism manifests itself under any of these guises makes little difference to its effects on individuals and society.

There can be, and have been, benign authoritarianisms, or authoritarianisms where the order and economic circumstances are such that the population largely accepts the situation and tacitly consents to it. The Spanish term '*dictablanda*', 'soft dictatorship', coined in the Franco era, is cognate to such expressions as 'enlightened absolutism' and 'benevolent dictatorship' (though Franco's dictatorship was not notably benevolent). Cited examples, such as the Antonine emperors of Rome of whom Marcus Aurelius was one, Hongwu the first emperor of the Ming dynasty in China, Catherine the Great of Russia, Kemal Ataturk of Turkey, and Josip Tito of Yugoslavia, were themselves not always quite so benign either, and in any case bring to mind the telling insight of Han Fei, the Legalist philosopher of the Warring States period in China (third century BCE):

> Han Fei believed that the age of sage kings was long over, and that it was pointless hoping that another would come along. He tells the story of a farmer who was ploughing a field in which there stood a tree. A hare racing through the field collided with the tree, broke its neck and died. The farmer so enjoyed eating the hare that he thereafter set aside his plough and sat and waited for another hare to come along and break its neck. The folly of doing the same in hopes of another sage king to appear, said Han Fei, speaks for itself.[20]

In the pre-classical epoch of ancient Greece the term 'tyrant' (*tyrannos*) was a neutral expression denoting an absolute ruler of a city-state or similar polity, but by the time of Plato and Aristotle, both of whom regarded tyranny as the worst form of government, the force of the truth that 'absolute power corrupts absolutely' was too obvious to deny. In ancient Rome when a military emergency occurred, a 'dictator' – literally 'one who says what is to be done' – was temporarily appointed to deal with the crisis. An example is Quintus Fabius Maximus Verrucosus, known as Cunctator ('delayer, postponer') – the term 'Fabian' is derived from him to denote one who takes a gradualist approach to solving problems – who was appointed when Hannibal invaded Italy with his elephants in the third century BCE, initiating a fifteen-year struggle that nearly proved fatal to Rome. Fabius' delaying tactics and avoidance of pitched battle eventually proved successful, but only after various of his political rivals had usurped his authority, rushed into major battles, and lost them – upon which he was recalled. Roman dictators were, however, restrained by a number of provisions; their appointment was temporary, they were not allowed to ride on horseback (a military precaution), and they could be dismissed by the Senate at any point.

Fabius is an example from the Republican period in Roman history. In the period of the Roman Empire after Augustus the examples of Caligula and Nero stand out as stark examples of tyrants, bearing witness to the lesson long before learned by Han Fei and Plato.

As Han Fei's allegory of the hare shows, the fact that there have been benevolent dictators is a lucky accident, and does nothing to recommend authoritarianism. Authoritarianism's key negatives of subverting or displacing the rule of law and of suppressing rights and civil liberties is enough to explain why. Placing rationally devised and agreed laws above the whims and ambitions of would-be rulers, as a restraint on power and limitation of its corrupting tendencies, is crucial to there being even half a chance of justice and individual flourishing in society. Neither of these two latter desiderata have ever been *fully* achieved anywhere, but in authoritarian states they are not even to the point. In these latter, equality among the ruled invariably manifests as all but the rulers being equally lacking in rights and liberties, and individual flourishing takes the single form of economic benefits such as are enjoyed by many Chinese, who are happy to trade rights and liberties for material welfare.

THE ALTERNATIVE MODEL

Keep firmly in mind what the phrase 'rights and liberties' *means*. It means the right to equal treatment before the law, and to due process at law, which means freedom from arbitrary arrest and punishment and subjection to torture or degrading treatment. It means the freedom to make choices about occupation, marriage and family life; to associate with others with whom one shares interests or aims; to get reliable information; to have a say in what laws and rules one is to live under, and to dissent, oppose, or argue for alternatives to them. It means being able to express oneself freely both as to opinion and as to personal matters such as one's sexuality; to exercise one's conscience in matters of belief; and to have an inviolable realm of privacy. These are rights and liberties which are taken for granted in democracies; indeed – alongside the processes by which governments are formed – they are constitutive of them. They are not available, or at best only cosmetically and with strict limits, in authoritarian dispensations.

The idea of the *rule of law* lies at the heart of this. Yes, tyrannies can pass laws that embody and enact their tyranny – the infamous Nuremberg Laws of Nazi Germany are a paradigm case. These two laws, adopted at the annual Nuremberg Rally of the Nazi party in 1935 and titled the 'Reich Citizenship Law' and the 'Law for the Protection of German Blood and German Honour', forbade marriage and sexual relations between Jews and non-Jews, banned employment in Jewish households for German women under the age of forty-five (i.e. for women of child-bearing age), and distinguished 'citizens' (with citizenship rights) from 'state subjects' (with no citizenship rights) by saying only people with German blood could be citizens. An addendum to the law brought people of colour and Roma into the same category of non-citizens, defining Roma along with Jews as 'enemies of the race-based state'. The Nuremberg Laws consolidated what had already begun in the way of a party-led national boycott of Jewish businesses, expulsion of all 'non-Aryans' from the civil service, burning of books by Jewish authors, and intimidation and violence against Jewish individuals.[21] Within just a few years it led to the unbridled horror of the Holocaust.

There are many other instances of laws that violate human rights. The US's antebellum slave laws, Jim Crow laws in the southern US states up to the 1960s, and the apartheid laws of South Africa between 1948 and 1994 are other prime examples.[22]

The concept of the *rule of law*, as a principle for a society in which rights and liberties are respected and in relevant cases protected by law, rather than their violation being sanctioned by law, must therefore be distinguished from *rule by law*, which is what the Nuremberg Laws exemplify.[23] 'The rule of law' is an ethical concept; 'rule by law' is a legalistic one.

The force of saying that 'the rule of law' is an *ethical* concept touches on an important matter, which is this: ethical considerations are more inclusive than moral considerations in the sense that the key ethical question is about *ethos*, 'character' – asking, 'What sort of person should I be? How should I live? By what values should I guide my life?' – while moral questions are chiefly about how one relates to others, that is, how to act on one's duties and obligations to them. One's moral choices will flow from one's ethical stance, but the latter is broader because it is about what one *is* in general, while moral considerations are about what one *does* in the circumstances one finds oneself in. For example: to endeavour to be a generous person rests on understanding and accepting why generosity is a virtue, while what counts as a generous act depends on the circumstances inviting the act; the same act of (say) donating $5 to a homeless charity would be generous for a person of restricted means and rather otherwise for a billionaire.

Accordingly, the rule of law concerns the *character* of the state and society in which it operates, and one of the consequences of its being upheld is how, if at all, law relates to particular *moral* questions about such matters as abortion, capital punishment, sex and sexuality, adultery, divorce, unmarried couples living together, euthanasia, meat-eating, truth-telling in circumstances where harm could result, the limits of loyalty (whistleblowing), and other familiarly contested issues. In some societies these are subject to law, in other societies some or all of them are regarded as matters of private choice or conscience and the law is not used to intervene by means of prohibition, control or punishment. The contrast between a society that enforces religious observance by law and punishes adultery with the death penalty, and a society which leaves beliefs and private sexual behaviour to the consciences of individuals, is obviously very marked; and says much about their overall ethical outlook, their character, what sort of societies they are.

The idea of the rule of law has two aspects: principles and procedures. The former include the rights and liberties of individuals and their relation to society in general; the latter concern how these engage with the institutions of the state, such as government, policing and the judicial process. To say this is to take a stance in a debate, because some thinkers regard the rule of law as exclusively about procedures – the operation of government and the judicial system – while others regard it as essentially about the protection of rights and liberties by means of these procedures. That is, 'the rule of law' is taken by the latter to mean the protection of principles constitutive of a free, open and democratic society, and definitive of such a thing, while the former – call them 'proceduralists' – leave aside the question of what principles are at stake and concentrate only on how the society's norms, whatever they are, are administered.

But the problem with the proceduralist view is that it does not distinguish between a 'rule *of* law' dispensation and a 'rule *by* law' dispensation, and indeed tends rather towards the latter because it does not address the question of whether the laws are themselves justified, instead taking them as given and focusing exclusively on how they are applied. Determining whether laws are themselves justified requires examination of the principles that underlie them and on which they do or could impinge. Thus they directly relate to their ethical justification, and this can be seen by noting that the fundamental driver of the concept of the rule of law is that government and its organs must behave within a framework of laws that regulate how they exercise their powers, not leaving it to the whims, preferences or arbitrary discretion of individuals or parties in power. And why should whims, preferences and

THE ALTERNATIVE MODEL

arbitrariness be guarded against? Obviously, because they are fertile in possibilities for injustice, and injustice means violation of the rights of citizens – and therefore the rule of law is explicitly about protection of these rights from arbitrary power. And this entails that the concept of the rule of law defines a system in which government is accountable – and therefore transparent in its operations so that abuses of its power can be prevented and, when they occur, remedied; and in which the judiciary is independent and the judicial process has integrity. It also means that the press is unmuzzled, opposition and dissent are free, and individuals' private lives are left to their own choices subject to the proviso that they do not harm others (given an appropriate understanding of what 'harm' means).[24]

These points can be summarised by saying that the *rule of law* places law above politics, government and governors, while *rule by law* makes law an instrument of political and government power.

The term 'democracy' in its generic sense of a 'democratic system' is therefore in practice near-synonymous with the phrase 'the rule of law', and correlatively 'authoritarianism' exists when the rule of law is absent because the ruling power ignores, overrides or is superior to the law, bends it to its own purposes, and/or applies it arbitrarily and unevenly, thereby violating the rights of individuals.

This characterisation of the rule of law can be acknowledged even granting that its application does not always deliver justice. Laws are made prospectively to cover a generality of cases and circumstances, and individual cases might have outcomes that are conformable to law but offend a natural sense of justice. Sometimes a natural sense of justice defies the law; in jury trials in England in the eighteenth and nineteenth centuries the laws on theft were so harsh – a starving man could be hanged or transported for stealing a loaf of bread – that juries acquitted even when the case against a defendant was proved. But one implicit condition of the rule of law is that those who are subject to it will obey it, even when it works against them in cases where the sense of fairness is offended. On such agreements the good order of society depends. In a democracy, when laws offend a natural sense of justice too much or too often, they can be changed by opposition to them; in authoritarian arrangements, only those in charge can change the law, as they are the only ones who can make it.

Personal experience of living under an authoritarian regime, even as a largely protected foreign resident, is instructive. I did so for a year in China in the early 1980s, teaching at a higher education institution. My mail was opened, telephone tapped, movements monitored, visitors and contacts recorded, apartment regularly searched in my absence, every lecture reported on, travel within the country monitored and permission denied to visit certain areas in it. For the most part all this ranged between irritating and amusing, a luxury that a 'foreign expert' (such was the designation) enjoyed. The maids servicing the rooms in the foreign compound where we lived, the waiters in its restaurant, certain students in class, certain colleagues at the university, even taxi drivers, were party to the surveillance, handing in their reports.

THE ALTERNATIVE MODEL

Although personally safe, my anxiety for Chinese friends and colleagues turned out to be justified. A colleague and I anonymously wrote a book about the history of the CCP when, some years afterwards, he was a visiting scholar at Oxford, and one consequence was that he later spent several terms in prison. A couple with whom my partner and I became friendly were subjected to restrictions and loss of privileges. Another friend was warned to limit contact. These were glimpses into what life was like for them. Compared to their experience, mine in their country was benign. To live a whole life in the foetid atmosphere of suspicion and anxiety, even though my friends there were habituated to it and knew, or hoped they knew, what not to say and do and whom to trust, is suffocating.

Arbitrariness was a feature of the system. A small example, not unrelated to my presence at the Institute of Philosophy where I was a visiting professor, was a sudden order issued to it that the influence of a number of Western philosophers was to be publicly denounced, and 'self-criticism' sessions held by those who had devoted study to them. A list of names was supplied (it included some odd choices, such as Alvin Toffler, the businessman and futurologist famous for his 1970 book *Future Shock*), and on it was the name of one of my teachers at Oxford, A. J. Ayer. When I returned to the UK I went to see Ayer and told him of this. He was dismayed; in the 1950s he had been invited by the Chinese government to be an official visitor to the country and had been fêted while there, consequently regarding himself as in good standing in China. I thought it was rather an honour for him to be singled out in this way, much as I later came to feel on discovering that a number of my own books are banned in certain Gulf states. But he was upset by the news. It reinforced my sense of the excessive caution my Chinese friends had to exercise in behaving (teaching, writing) in ways they thought were acceptable, only to find that a sudden reversal of policy exposed them to criticism or worse.

In his book *On Tyranny* the Yale historian Timothy Snyder, writing about how to resist tyranny, says that the first commandment in doing so is, 'Do not obey in advance'.[25] The repressive Chinese regime obliged everyone to do exactly that. People had to hope they were obeying whatever they currently believed the authorities wanted of them. This meant having to police their very thoughts in case they said or did something inadvertently that could count as an act of disobedience. Because of sudden arbitrary reversals of policy, they knew they could always find themselves to be wrong and in trouble. It is one of the tricks of authoritarian regimes to keep everyone cowed and uncertain. At time of writing, matters in China are no different.[26] By a ghastly parallelism they appear to be, again at time of writing, the methodology preferred by the Trump administration that came into office in the US in January 2025.

It is, however and alas, not only in places like China and North Korea that people are under constant surveillance. The unrelenting need to perform the risky dance of 'advance obedience' does not, thankfully, impose its burden on most citizens of Western countries unless they are criminals, terrorists or illegal immigrants, but 'surveillance capitalism', potentiated by

THE ALTERNATIVE MODEL

our wholesale yielding of privacy to social media platforms, operates just as relentlessly. The phrase 'surveillance capitalism' comes from Shoshana Zuboff's *The Age of Surveillance Capitalism*, which dissects the way in which precisely articulated knowledge about who and what each one of us is is required by business for knowing how to sell us things.[27] If we thought that commercial enterprises are interested in this information only to sell us their products and services, and that this is as far as it goes, we would be naive. For not only do they sell us goods and services, they also sell our information to others, including political parties, and the information can be accessed or required by agencies of the state. Still worse, because this detailed and systematic system of surveillance already exists, it is tailor-made for abuse if an authoritarian regime comes to power. These words were written within days of news reports that Trump intended to use the military to carry out mass round-ups and deportations of immigrants in the US; one ready resource for identifying many of them exists in the emails, text messages or bank card purchases that can be used to track them down.[28] And this in a country that is vocal in its self-congratulation as a democracy.

The nature and methods of authoritarianism are anatomised in books by New York University historian Ruth Ben-Ghiat in *Strongmen* and journalist and historian Anne Applebaum in *Autocracy Inc*.[29] The key insight in the latter is stated at its outset:

> Nowadays, autocracies are run not by one bad guy but by sophisticated networks relying on kleptocratic financial

structures, a complex of security services – military, paramilitary, police – and technological experts who provide surveillance, propaganda, and disinformation. The members of these networks are connected not only to one another within a given autocracy but also to networks in other autocratic countries, and sometimes in democracies too. Corrupt, state-controlled companies in one dictatorship do business with corrupt, state-controlled companies in another … The propagandists share resources – the troll farms and media networks that promote one dictator's propaganda can also be used to promote another's – as well as themes: the degeneracy of democracy, the stability of autocracy, the evil of America.[30]

An example at time of writing of overt collaboration between autocracies is how North Korea and Iran support Russia in the attack it launched on Ukraine in February 2022, escalating a conflict that began with Russia's invasions and annexations of the Crimea and the Donbas region of eastern Ukraine, both in 2014 – a collaboration involving military hardware from Iran, troops from North Korea, and financial and trade facilitations from China and certain other BRICs+ countries.[31] As Applebaum points out, mutualities between autocracies are not restricted to military aid. They take a number of other forms, not least in economic and financial respects. She writes:

> Since 2008, the United States, Canada, and the European Union have ramped up sanctions on Venezuela in response to the regime's brutality, drug smuggling, and links to international

crime. Yet President Nicolás Maduro's regime receives loans from Russia, which also invests in Venezuela's oil industry, as does Iran. A Belarussian company assembles tractors in Venezuela. Turkey facilitates the illicit Venezuelan gold trade. Cuba has long provided security advisers and security technology to its counterparts in Caracas. Chinese-made water cannons, tear-gas canisters, and shields were used to crush street protesters in Caracas in 2014 and again in 2017, leaving more than seventy dead, while Chinese-designed surveillance technology is used to monitor the public.[32]

And then there is the aid that autocrats give to would-be autocrats in currently democratic countries in order to overthrow their governments from within by the more sophisticated means they have learned since the days of military coups. We see 'influence media and elite audiences around the world; carefully curated Russian propaganda campaigns, some amplified by both paid and unpaid members of the American and European far right … Antidemocratic rhetoric has gone global.'[33] The anti-democratic rhetoric campaign has found social media platforms, and the internet in general, a gift of gold.[34] Its goals, as noted in connection with Bannon's 'Movement' described earlier, are not secret.

What is it that authoritarians want? To get and keep power it seems that they are prepared to see their countries suffer and decline economically and socially. Vladimir Putin's warmongering has cost scores of thousands of lives, most of them Russian, and despite financial support from other autocracies has damaged Russia's economy. Nicolás Maduro of Venezuela is a classic example of a dictator in the most literal sense of the term, overturning the governing structures of the country to rule by decree, taking down what was once South America's richest country to being the continent's poorest, scarred by thousands of extrajudicial killings and brutal suppression of dissent, driving seven million Venezuelans to seek refuge outside its borders.[35] In Maduro's case personal power-hunger appears to override every other consideration. In Putin's case there is an additional factor: irredentism, the desire to recover for Russia what it lost after the collapse of the Soviet Union, together with fear – fear of the encroachment of NATO and the European Union upon Russia's borders, perceived as a threat because that is the only lens through which Putin views geopolitics.

Putin's imperial ambition is the same as China's desire to recover -- perhaps, in such cases as Tibet, indeed in all cases, 'recover' with inverted commas is the better way of putting it – domains it historically possessed. Authoritarian rulers in history have been ambitious to extend their domains in order to command greater resources of people and material wealth, and to overmaster perceived threats to their current hold on power. In the irredentist expansionism of Russia and China, but also in the global reach of US military and economic power premised on security and foreign policy imperatives, contemporary geopolitics rings loud with history's echoes. In the US case this has hitherto chiefly been carried out by means of 'informal empire'; Trump's ambitions with regard to Greenland, Canada and the Panama Canal move the US into the Russia–Ukraine, China–Taiwan camp.[36]

THE ALTERNATIVE MODEL

In history it was principally troops and weapons that carried out the work of getting and maintaining empire, though spying, propaganda and subversion were always part of the arsenal. Over two thousand years ago Sun Tzu said, in his *Art of War*, that 'the supreme art of war is to subdue the enemy without fighting' – by 'fighting' he meant physical fighting; but use of the weapons of propaganda and subversion constitutes fighting in a different guise. In the digital age it has become as much a front-line endeavour as missiles, drones and uniformed human bodies. In the war of ideas they wage, anti-democratic agencies, whether they are states like Russia from without or right-wing movements within, flood social media with a variety of tactics, from outright apologetics for their causes to subtle and cumulative suggestions, untruths, misinformation and influence, not least recruitment of followers by social media influencers. Influencers and fellow-travellers are especially useful; deploying them to insinuate an anti-democratic agenda drop by drop manifests the technique denoted in the Chinese saying, 'borrowing boats to reach the sea'.[37]

Democracy is being assailed from so many sides and in so many ways that the illusion that authoritarian and would-be authoritarian leaders wish to create, namely, that populism is a spontaneous movement rising from the grassroots, has persuaded many. It is true enough that there are sections of society affected by social and economic injustices and that too many aspects of capitalism, and the austerity measures that either directly or indirectly protect it, cause the injustices. The disaffection of these groups is both understandable and in itself justified as regards the impact on living standards, which are the most immediate sore point. The disaffection is exploited by populist politicians who inflame it deliberately by directing its ire at targets that suit the populist politicians' aims: immigrants, 'the liberal elite', the democratic order itself interpreted as a system designed to serve the interests of an 'establishment'. These politicians are careful not to mention that the alternative they offer involves diminishing or extinguishing the rights and liberties, the protection of the rule of law, from which everyone benefits in a democratic order.

But when these latter consequences materialise, popular movements turn out to be rather different from those hoped for by authoritarian politicians. An example is what happened in Bangladesh, as Larry Diamond reports in an essay in *Foreign Affairs*.[38] The country's leader, Sheikh Hasina, who ruled for the fifteen years between 2009 and 2024, had increasingly assumed control over 'the courts, prosecutors, government agencies, and the police, using them to silence the media, persecute her opponents, cow private business, and subvert the institutions and traditions that previously allowed for reasonably free and fair elections.'[39] The Bangladeshi people reacted to this illiberalism by ousting Hasina in 2024 in a civil disobedience campaign, itself sparked by violent assaults on demonstrators in which hundreds were killed, thousands injured and 10,000 arrested. The straw that broke the camel's back, provoking the demonstrations, was yet another step in Hasina's extension of control: the introduction of a quota system for civil service jobs that favoured her supporters. Students took to the streets to protest the measure, and Hasina ordered a brutal crackdown. Within months the populace's reaction to the crackdown triggered her downfall.

The trajectory of Bangladesh under Hasina is a model of what happens when authoritarians take control.

> Corrupt leaders have hollowed out democratic institutions and established authoritarian rule behind the façade of multiparty elections. Following a common playbook, they wholly dismantled democracy in El Salvador, Hungary, Nicaragua, Serbia, Tunisia, Turkey, and Venezuela. Elsewhere, similar tools have been used to degrade democracy ... recent examples include Georgia, Honduras, India, Indonesia, the Philippines, and Sri Lanka.[40]

Meanwhile a number of other countries occupy a 'halfway house' where constitutional norms have been violated but the population 'will not tolerate the complete elimination of individual freedoms, civic pluralism, multiparty elections, and at least the possibility of parties alternating in power' – examples are Kenya and Tanzania.[41]

The fact that 'populism' leading to authoritarian rule is a top-down not bottom-up phenomenon is stressed by Larry M. Bartels in an essay in the same issue of *Foreign Affairs*:

> As the eminent political scientist E. E. Schattschneider observed several decades ago, this sort of understanding [of populism *versus* democracy] is 'essentially simplistic, based on a tremendously exaggerated notion of the immediacy and urgency of the

connection of public opinion and events.' The fate of democracy lies in the hands of politicians. It is they who choose to manage, mollify, ignore or inflame populist sentiment. It is a dangerous blunder to gullibly accept their show of bowing to the ostensible will of the people. And when popular grievances are used as a pretext for bad policy – or, even worse, as a pretext for democratic backsliding – it is politicians, not the citizenry, who are culpable.[42]

In the interest of protecting civil liberties, human rights and the rule of law, opposing authoritarianism in any of its guises is a necessity as obvious as it is urgent. And that means that politics and politicians have to be subjected to the rule of law, by being constitutionally prevented from usurping it: see chapter 5.

The means by which 'democratic backsliding' into authoritarianism happens follows a clear, well-understood programme, a 'playbook'. Paradigm cases of its implementation are provided by Viktor Orbán in Hungary, Donald Trump in the US at time of writing, and – though some are too hesitant to draw the parallel, perhaps in shocked disbelief that it is happening again – Hitler's Germany in the 1930s.

It begins with popularist capture of the democratic process, made easier if the structures of the democracy are manipulable because of the factors described in these pages. Once in power, an authoritarian entity – whether an individual helped by compliant lieutenants or a party machine – having already laid the groundwork in the rhetoric used to gain a base of support, sets to work as follows.

THE ALTERNATIVE MODEL

It politicises the agencies of government and independent state bodies by getting rid of staff seen as unsympathetic to its agenda, replacing them with its own people, typically posting its cronies in the highest positions. It weakens the judiciary, and controls what can be taught in educational institutions. Within the first months of the second Trump presidency this process had either happened or begun with the Department of Justice, the FBI, the Federal Reserve (central bank), the Federal Communications Commission, the Federal Trade Commission's Bureau of Consumer Protection, the Department of Health and Human Services, the Department of Education, and others.[43]

The authoritarian entity spreads misinformation and disinformation, and aids the proliferation of both by quashing dissent, interfering with mainstream media organisations by bullying them, censoring them, denying them licenses to operate, threatening journalists or suborning them, and by lifting controls on the requirements for truth, fact and limiting of hate speech on social media platforms (see the next chapter).[44] In the US this has been easy because the platforms are controlled by a small group of ultra-rich individuals who have aligned themselves with the Trump machine because they stand to profit thereby. Control of the flow of information, and in places such as Russia, China – an egregious case – Hungary and elsewhere (even, to a degree, in the UK), using state-controlled media as propaganda outlets, allows distortions or outright falsehoods to be disseminated. The US and Hungary are examples of putative democracies where disinformation about vulnerable populations, not least immigrants and other minorities, is used to demonise and scapegoat them as the source of the problems faced by disaffected groups. Misinformation becomes the main message, and is a powerful tool for distracting the populace, polarising it and redirecting its disaffections towards scapegoats and the authoritarian regime's opponents.

The authoritarian entity encourages or condones violence by groups (*vide* 'January 6' insurrectionists who attacked the Capitol in Washington; 'Kristallnacht' in Germany in November 1938) which support the authoritarian entity, and itself uses threatening rhetoric against individuals (*vide* Trump's verbal attacks on e.g. Liz Cheney and Hillary Clinton) and groups (*vide* the Nazis and Jews) which in most cases of the historical unfolding of this process has resulted, sooner or later, in actual attacks, imprisonment or murder.[45] It uses the military against protestors and in rounding up people to be deported or detained.

It aggrandises the leader or the party, concentrates powers in its hands, and weakens or dismantles constitutional checks to the exercise of its power.

It corrupts the electoral process by changing the rules, denying the vote to specified groups, even lying about the outcome and claiming overwhelming support.

The authoritarian entity's direct aim is to weaken civil society, stifle opposition, mobilise its base as a supplementary force for controlling the state, undermine the rule of law in order to be above the law, control information, control the instruments of coercion (police and military), and thereby to remain permanently in power. An outright coup can effect all this in a single night; in cases of 'democratic backsliding' as in Hungary and (at time of writing) the US, the coup is a process, though – aided by a following wind, blown by the cumulative effect of the rise of far-right politics in a number of democracies – the US process has been faster than in Hungary.[46]

How is this process to be opposed? The advice of Maria Ressa, the Filipino journalist and campaigner who was awarded the 2021 Nobel Peace Prize for her fight against the Philippine dictator Rodrigo Duterte, is clear (I paraphrase):

> What you do straight away matters; every day you do nothing you get weaker – you have to ask yourself what you are prepared to sacrifice – you have to defend the facts, the truth, and your rights: you have to draw a line. Collaborate with others in the endeavour, organise with civil society groups, do not be indifferent to what is happening to others such as vilification or oppression of targeted groups. Oppose authoritarian tendencies at every turn. Do not 'obey in advance'. Keep information flowing: authoritarians have to 'control the message' to stay in power. Above all, focus on what needs to be done: *every day you do nothing you get weaker*; act before the process gets too far.[47]

It might seem, to the isolated individual, that this is a very tall order. But one should not underestimate the power of individuals and communities of interest. After all, the authoritarians themselves did it – though admittedly they had money and convenient pre-positioning on their side. But what is the option – to succumb? No, and forever No. Therefore one has to ask what one is prepared to do, what one is prepared to sacrifice. The mantra has to be: *Do not obey in advance. Every day you do nothing you get weaker. Resist by every morally legitimate and principled means: but resist, and never give up.*

4

INTERFERENCE UNDERMINING DEMOCRACY

In the first years of the twenty-first century the threat not just to democracies but to any society anywhere was seen as religiously motivated terrorism, taking the form of acts of mass-murder atrocity attacks on large commercial or government buildings, railway stations, market places and airplanes. This, though it is no comfort to say so, was an extension of something familiar; in the nineteenth century anarchists set off bombs, and in all periods there have been assassinations, most of these occurrences political in intent. Some of them triggered epoch-making changes to history; teenager Gavrilo Princip's assassination of Archduke Franz Ferdinand of Austria on 28 June 1914 was the immediate trigger for the First World War, which sharply dog-legged history into almost everything that has happened in world affairs since.

The attack on the Twin Towers in New York and the Pentagon in Washington on 11 September 2001, '9/11', was a ghastly chapter in the same story. The means were different, but in *kind* it was the same. Amid distractions from the fallout from this – the Iraq and Afghanistan wars, further Islamist terror attacks in London and Madrid, the self-imposed restrictions on civil liberties in states regarding themselves as targets in the hope of exchanging freedoms for security[1] – a new and even greater threat was brewing. This was the advent of social media, use made by extremist movements from both inside and outside democracies of wider possibilities offered by the internet, and exploitation of the openness of democracies themselves to insert subversive factors.

By the end of the first decade of the twenty-first century social media platforms had rapidly progressed both in their adoption and their virality. Anyone with Facebook or Twitter could offer their opinion to the world, campaign and advocate – sometimes for good causes, often to spread rumours, conspiracy theories and untruths. When the internet became universal in the 1990s there was a joyous hope that it would promote a global democracy in which gate-keepers to information were swept aside and there could be open debate and sharing both of ideas and of news unedited by partisan interests. How naive we were: for, as we have all seen to our cost, despite the good things that the internet has brought, it has become and remained, chiefly in the form of the social media platforms on it, as much if not more a sewer of hate speech, lies and lunacies that by their ill-effects and volume have polluted and too often drowned the good things.

Social media, in particular, potentiated this. It creates silos and echo chambers in which people congregate to have their prejudices reinforced hourly. It has been a godsend to far-left and far-right messaging, to 'influencers', 'trolls' and haters cloaked in anonymity, venting their resentments. The bile, ignorance and threat displayed in the vomitus of responses that appear on so many 'threads' posted on social media is alarming; for some, terrifying. One acquaintance, after giving a streamed talk on certain feminist issues, received messages threatening her with rape, an arson attack on her home, and hope that her children would die of horrible diseases. And this was by no means an unusual event, but par for the course in her experience.

Personal attacks have become a mere cost of inhabiting the social media universe, which for practical reasons few can now leave. Social media 'pile-ons' in culture war settings have taken such attacks into a wider domain, with public accusations, shaming, 'doxing', and calls to 'cancel' individuals or institutions.[2] These attacks come not only from people on the opposed side of some issue, but from people on the same side who hold more vehement versions of the position in question and regard moderates as traitors to the cause.[3]

But the most general threat is to democracy itself, because the spread of distortions, exaggerations and misinformation promoting mistrust and deepening divisions in society is more dangerous than personalised venom from unpleasant people, whether the danger arises from an un-orchestrated result of mutual inflammations in echo chambers, or a deliberate campaign by extremist political movements both internally and by external state agencies like Russia, which is a major player in this endeavour. Most people now get their news or 'news' via their social media, filtered through the lens of the 'bot'- and 'troll'-infested echo chambers they are in, no attention being paid to different views or correctives, with no debate and no evaluation of competing perspectives.

Social media platform providers such as Meta (formerly Facebook) dispute the claim that their platforms increase polarisation. That claim is in turn challenged by social scientist Jonathan Haidt on the basis of extensive research in collaboration with other analysts.[4] Haidt acknowledges that social media is not the only conduit of anti-democratic activity and not the only cause of it: in the US, in addition to the radicalisation of the Republican Party in the 1990s and the relentless partisanship of Fox News, there are other complex factors:

> including the growing politicization of the urban-rural divide; rising immigration; the increasing power of big and very partisan donors; the loss of a common enemy when the Soviet Union collapsed; and the loss of the 'Greatest Generation' which had an ethos of service forged in the crisis of the Second World War. And although polarization rose rapidly in the 2010s, the rise began in the 90s, so I cannot pin the *majority* of the rise on social media.[5]

But since the advent of hyper-viral social media at the end of the twenty-first century's first decade there have been 'ever nastier cross-party relationships', the culture wars have spread a 'fearful dynamic' to 'newsrooms, companies, non-profit organisations, and many other parts of society', and the echo chambers of social media groups inflame partisanship: 'When affective polarization is high, partisans tolerate antidemocratic behaviour by politicians on their own side – such as the January 6 attack on the US Capitol'.[6]

What has happened in these respects in the US has happened in the UK and elsewhere, for closely similar reasons and with identical outcomes.

In these increasing divisions, deliberate intervention from outside finds fertile ground. A telling analysis is provided by the National Endowment for Democracy in a 2017 study by a team drawn from the US, Latin America, Poland and Slovakia.[7] The authors of the introductory essay introduce the concept of 'sharp power' as a more apt label than 'soft power' for activities of influence and propaganda.

> Over the past decade, China and Russia have spent billions of dollars to shape public opinion and perceptions around the world, employing a diverse toolkit that includes thousands of people-to-people exchanges, wide-ranging cultural activities, educational programs (most notably the ever-expanding network of controversial Confucius Institutes), and the development of media enterprises and information initiatives with global reach. As memory of the Cold War era receded, analysts, journalists, and policymakers in the democracies came to see authoritarian influence efforts through the familiar lens of 'soft power.' But some of the most visible authoritarian influence techniques used by countries such as China and Russia, while not 'hard' in the openly coercive and especially military sense, are not really 'soft' either.[8]

Accordingly the authors introduce the notion of 'sharp power' to denote 'authoritarian influence efforts [that] are "sharp" in the sense that they pierce, penetrate, or perforate the information and political environments in the targeted countries'.[9]

This is especially so in relatively new and still vulnerable democracies where democratic practices have not yet deepened their roots, securing the civil liberties and the effective rule of law that embodies or protects them. Whereas soft power outreach was typically aimed at winning hearts and minds, sharp power seeks to:

> influence their target audiences by manipulating or distorting the information that reaches them ... the attempt by Beijing and Moscow to wield influence through initiatives in the spheres of media, culture, think tanks, and academia is neither a 'charm offensive' nor an effort to 'win hearts and minds,' the common frame of reference for 'soft power' efforts. This authoritarian influence is not principally about attraction or even persuasion; instead, it centres on distraction and manipulation. These ambitious authoritarian regimes, which systematically suppress political pluralism and free expression at home, are increasingly seeking to apply similar principles internationally to secure their interests.[10]

There are differences of tone in the approaches taken by Moscow and Beijing, but:

> both stem from an ideological model that privileges state power over individual liberty and is fundamentally hostile to free expression, open debate, and independent thought. At the same time, both Beijing and Moscow clearly take advantage of the

openness of democratic systems ... China has spent tens of billions of dollars to shape public opinion and perceptions around the world ... During roughly the same period, the Russian government accelerated its own efforts in this sphere. In the mid-2000s, the Kremlin launched the global television network Russia Today (since rebranded as the more unassuming 'RT'), built up its capacity to manipulate content online, increased its support for state-affiliated policy institutes, and more generally cultivated a web of influence activities – both on and offline – designed to alter international views to its advantage.[11]

This activity extends to interference in elections and suborning of politicians. During the 2024 election campaign in the US, three government departments – Treasury, State and Justice – combined to 'aggressively counter' Russian efforts to interfere, among other things charging RT with paying $10 million to a Tennessee firm 'to create and distribute content to US audiences with hidden Russian government messaging'.[12] The British Conservative Party and a number of its individual Members of Parliament received substantial donations from Russian-linked sources – among them the wife of a former finance minister under Putin – as did campaigners for Brexit in 2016, one of whom, Nigel Farage, was a highly frequent regular on RT.[13] In the UK case the Russian links with the right wing in politics have an extensive history; as a financial centre for not-always-clean money the City of London handles over £27 billion of Russian investments, for which the estimated £2 million donated by Russia-linked individuals to Boris Johnson's party, after he took office in 2019, appears a highly economical cost of business.[14]

As the 'sharp power' study indicated, interference efforts by Russia are widespread. Its direct interference in elections in Georgia and Moldova in the early 2020s are salient examples.[15] It channelled money to the Brexit 'Leave' campaign in 2016, and additionally spent up to £4 million on a pro-'Leave' media influence campaign through RT and the Russian state-owned news agency Sputnik, as detailed in a report to the Culture, Media and Sport select committee of the House of Commons.[16] Another and in many ways more pertinent Parliamentary body, the Intelligence and Security Committee, concluded that Russian interference in UK politics is commonplace; publication of its report, stating that 'Russian influence in the UK is the new normal ... the UK is clearly a target for Russian disinformation', was blocked by Boris Johnson's government, his party recipient of Russian donations.[17]

> Crucially, the UK Government is accused of making a deliberate effort not to find out how Russian influence may have affected the June 2016 Brexit vote. This is all the more incredible because the government admits there was Russian interference in the 2014 Scottish referendum, declaring it the first time that Russia directly interfered in a Western election. The government also admits that Russia interfered in the December 2019 [UK] general election.[18]

These are merely a few examples of known or credibly suspected Russian interference.

INTERFERENCE UNDERMINING DEMOCRACY

One of China's sharp power tools is its Confucius Institutes, with over nine million students at 525 centres in 146 countries and regions. There are more than 100 Confucius Institutes in the US alone, along with a further 500 Confucius Classrooms at US elementary and high schools.

> Confucius Institutes, financed by the Chinese government and supervised by the Chinese Communist Party, are moulding attitudes about China, painting an idyllic portrait in which Mao Zedong is a revolutionary hero and the Tiananmen Square massacre never happened. That the Confucius Institutes are instruments of propaganda was confirmed by Li Changchun, the head of propaganda for the Chinese Communist Party, who boasted that the Institutes were 'an important part of China's overseas propaganda setup'.[19]

In 2019 the BBC reported that:

> to its critics the [Chinese] government-run body – which offers language and cultural programmes overseas – is a way for Beijing to spread propaganda under the guise of teaching, interfere with free speech on campuses and even to spy on students. In recent weeks, a flurry of universities around the world have shut down programmes operated by the institute. And in Australia, an investigation is even under way into whether agreements between universities and the institute have broken anti-foreign interference laws.[20]

Add the economic influence exerted by China in South America, South Asia and Africa where investment and the stationing of personnel in commercial operations reprises the way Western countries used and still use commercial operations and military bases to influence countries abroad.[21] In the nineteenth century the practice of establishing footholds in China with extraterritorial status – Hong Kong, Shanghai and Tianjin are major examples – through financial muscle influenced (and, in that case, with the threat and occasional application of military power also) the policies of the state. In describing China's 'Belt and Road Initiative' Xi Jinping's assertion that its aim is to create a 'community of common destiny' was intended to suggest that the benefits would be mutually economic, but the phrase admits of other readings.[22]

On one view the relatively benign economic reading of Xi's remark is plausible; China's manufacturing overproduction requires it to create markets for its products abroad. To export its steel, aluminium and concrete it invests in mining and construction in receptively money-starved countries. By doing so it has become Africa's biggest partner in trade. But the trade has come with strings attached, not least through the credit extended, 'trapping numerous countries in unsustainable levels of debt'.[23] The trade imbalance works against the host countries, from which China extracts raw materials and in return sends cheap and often shoddy goods that undermine local manufacture. For just two examples: China offered Guinea a loan twice the size of that country's GDP in order to dominate its reserves of bauxite, needed for China's aluminium industry; in Zambia China has taken over the copper mining industry, sending its own workers and equipment and prompting observers to state that 'the influx of the Chinese ... will threaten the sovereignty and security of the country'.[24] Unemployment for many local workers, and inattention to health and safety protections affecting others, have caused unrest in both places, which the local governments are obliged to quell on China's behalf.

Among the intended effects of this activity is the subversion of democracy. Of course Moscow and Beijing (and other players, such as Iran) also seek to influence perceptions of their states, to mitigate criticism and protect business relations, but achieving a positive perception of themselves goes alongside criticism of democracies as inefficient, effete, unequal and morally corrupt. To secure its operations abroad China does not tolerate challenge to its activities of the kind that an open society not only permits but encourages through its traditions and institutions. An authoritarian regime that can exert as much control over its population as China does at home suits it best.

Achieving this is relatively easy in young, poor and vulnerable states. But China and Russia also seek to destabilise and weaken the older democracies – the US and European states which between them still retain a major influence in world affairs. Russia perceives NATO and the EU as its greatest threats, and works to divide them as international bodies; one main effort to achieve this is to undermine attitudes to them within member states. Brexit is an example of a success for Russia in this respect, and it works hard trying to fragment the EU further. At time of writing it appears to be succeeding in its aim of weakening the NATO alliance as Trump does its work for it in Washington.[25] China is an economic superpower, and seeks to be more. By fomenting division with the Western democracies it seeks to enfeeble their opposition to its ambition to exert hegemony in the Asia-Pacific region and, thereafter, beyond.

China, Russia and other authoritarian regimes attack democracy by undermining its credentials, impugning human rights, emphasising weaknesses, and claiming that it is the democracies which – as a joint communiqué by Russia and China stated on the eve of Russia's 2022 invasion of Ukraine – constitute 'serious threats to global and regional peace and stability and undermine the stability of the world order.'[26] Yet at the same time both states are hard at work, leading:

> a boom in transnational repression – actions against dissidents and critics in other countries ... Russia is expert at poisonings and assassinations, while China specialises in intimidation and threats, often coordinated by diplomats, as well as forced repatriations ... in addition to achieving their goal of silencing their critics, they see the benefit of undermining confidence in democratic institutions, law enforcement, and public morale.[27]

Inadvertently or otherwise, the authoritarian regimes are helped by banks and investment companies, accountants, lobbying firms, media outlets, public relations and marketing companies, social media influencers and politicians, within democracies themselves.[28] The openness of democracies provides many points of entry for the insertion of influence and manipulation, misinformation and disruption. Not only can division and dissent be exploited, they can be created; using 'bots' to inflame both sides of a dispute simultaneously raises the stakes and distracts as well as divides. Infiltrating activist organisations to stir them up further even to the point of violent action is a familiar method. The fact that agents and fellow travellers of authoritarian regimes can invest in business and buy property, including homes, in democracies gives them one kind of ready platform; the internet and social media give them yet greater leverage, global and unremitting, for achieving the same end. The mainstreaming of hate speech and bitter political rivalries on social media platforms is both a gift to and a gift from the deliberate campaign to undermine democracy; and it is working.

Ironically, while undermining the concept of democracy as it is understood and operates in Western liberal polities, Beijing claims that China is itself democratic, indeed that its 'whole-process people's democracy' is 'true democracy'. Russia's 1993 Constitution (amended in 2008 and 2014 but most significantly in 2020 to strengthen yet further Putin's hold on power) nominally made the Russian Federation a democracy, and in the chaotic Yeltsin years – Boris Yeltsin was President of Russia from 1991 to 1999 – something like a multiparty system obtained; but by the beginning of the twenty-first century the *nomenklatura* were back in power and no democratic transition had occurred, only the outward forms persisting cosmetically while rapid 'autocratic reconsolidation' took place.[29]

Consider each of these in turn.

The 're-autocratisation' of Russia after the collapse of the Soviet Union happened very quickly. The prospect of democracy taking root in the new Russian Federation was stymied early by Yeltsin's suppression of political opposition and the 1993 Constitution's embedding of centralised executive power. When Yeltsin handed over to the then unknown ex-KGB lieutenant colonel Vladimir Putin in 1999, conditions were ripe for the latter to extinguish such flickerings of democracy as there had been. Most of the structures of the Soviet state were still in place, and none of the processes distinctive of a democratic order – tolerated political plurality and competition, the rule of law, freedom of expression, peaceful transition of power through fair elections – took place. Yet more, the personnel of the Soviet order were still in position, and ensured that no competing political elite emerged. The pattern was the same in the new states created by the Soviet Union's collapse:

> countries that were bereft of powerful democrats at transition time – the former Soviet republics of Azerbaijan, Kazakhstan, Turkmenistan and Uzbekistan fell into this class – saw democratic practices gain little or no ground, while autocratic reconsolidation was swift. Across the post-Soviet space, the more likely a country was to elect members or associates of the old Soviet *nomenklatura* to post-communist offices, the more likely was it also to experience a reversal of any movement toward democracy.[30]

What happened on the political and constitutional front in Russia was a fire; the petrol thrown on it was the economic reforms of Yeltsin's Prime Minister, Yegor Gaidar, who ended controls on prices and trade and sold off state assets, intending to effect a 'shock' transition to a free-market economy. What happened was the creation of billionaire oligarchs, members of the Soviet *nomenklatura* who were perfectly positioned to snap up formerly state-controlled enterprises for a song, and heads of enterprises who privatised them while they were still in control.[31] With their influence in the state, these formidably powerful elements blocked further attempts at reform. By the time Putin was in power he was able to eliminate:

> power centers that had emerged when the federal center was weak. He reinstituted control over the regions, coopted the private sector and independent media, repressed opponents, and manipulated elections ... The response of Russia's political elites to Putin's re-autocratization was euphoric. To them, it meant that clear and familiar rules of the game were back – the future had become predictable again ... The old Soviet *nomenklatura*, steeped in antidemocratic norms and habits, remained atop the Russian political system and preserved many formal and informal institutions of the *ancien regime*.[32]

In some former Soviet bloc states strong democrats were able to resist the inertial drag of the apparatchik structure; Václav Havel in Czechoslovakia is an outstanding example. But Russia today is scarcely distinguishable from its Soviet avatar as an autocratic state. Add to this the passionate irredentism of Putin, intent on reclaiming as much of the territory and influence in Eastern Europe and Central Asia that the Soviet

Union once held, and one sees an inflammatory mixture. In 2008 he attacked Georgia, detaching South Ossetia and Abkhazia from it. In 2014 he invaded and captured the Crimea. His prosecution of the Chechnya campaign, officially announced as 'completed' in 2017, was brutal even by the standards of all-out war. The February 2022 invasion of Ukraine was another and this time far more dangerous chapter in the same story. Even leaving aside Putin's relations with Iran, China, North Korea and Syria, his irredentism and aggressive opposition to the threat he perceives from NATO and EU expansion provide the context for Russia's vigorous prosecution of a cyber-war against all whom it regards as enemies.[33] Undermining Western states with disinformation, stirring divisions, inserting the Russian perspective into messaging, bombarding social media with bots and trolls, go alongside employing sympathisers within the democracies, financing politicians and media outlets, inserting presence through oligarchs who own residential and commercial properties, businesses, football clubs and other assets, in Western countries. All are part of what is an actual ongoing state of already-existing war between Russia and its perceived enemies.[34]

China mounts its challenge in similar ways, though at time of writing without actual military interventions if one discounts the establishment of military bases in the Spratly Islands and rapid enhancement of its armed forces.[35]

China's response to US President Joe Biden's 'Summit for Democracy' initiative encapsulates its counter-offensive. On taking office in 2020 Biden made a speech in which he identified China's rising power as a 'special challenge' because it is 'playing the long game by extending its global reach, promoting its own political model, and investing in the technologies of the future'.[36] Accordingly in 2021 he hosted the first Summit for Democracy, a virtual conference whose themes were 'defending against authoritarianism, fighting corruption and advancing respect for human rights'.[37] A second summit in 2023, hosted by the US with Zambia, South Korea, Costa Rica and the Netherlands, and a third hosted by South Korea, followed.

The first summit was bitterly criticised by China, accusing it of promoting a 'Cold War mentality' and representing 'nothing but an attempt to divide the world into opposing political camps and advance the US' own strategic agenda with democracy as an excuse'.[38] Contrasting itself with Western democracies, China claimed that not only is it a democracy itself but it is a 'true democracy', positioning the contrast not as between democracies and autocracies, but between different conceptions of democracy.[39] China thus contests the general Western attitude to it as 'undemocratic, illiberal, and autocratic' by 'proactively ... promoting its idea of democracy to domestic and international audiences' – and its idea is 'whole-process people's democracy', the new term for 'dictatorship of the proletariat', which means that the people *as a collective* (i.e. as a single body, not through a sum-over-individual-choices-made as in a Western election) rule through the leadership of the CCP.[40] At the same time China advocates recognisably liberal democratic ideals of 'freedom, equality, inclusiveness, multilateralism, and sovereignty' for the *international* order, which Beijing sees as itself a domain of democracy.⁴¹ Beijing's charge against the US is that it does not espouse these values in international affairs.

The organisation of China's argument is interesting. It begins by criticising the way US democracy operates in practice.

> As shown in the Capitol riots in 2021, the political polarization in the United States that is intensified by partisan politics currently seems irreconcilable, implying that American multi-party democracy invites only endless identity politics and social rifts which produce a perpetual conflict … [accordingly] the United States is no longer a beacon of democracy in the 21st century… plutocracy is another essential feature of American democracy … '[i]n the US, money is the breast milk of politics and elections increasingly morph into monologues of the wealthy, while the public call for democracy is made only "a jarring note." With the devil of money lurking in every corner of American politics, fairness and justice is naturally strained' … American democracy today is thus a money-driven political culture which does not reflect the interests of the people and the nation, widening the gap between the rich and poor.⁴²

Moreover, 'the Supreme Court almost always makes decisions in favor of Christian evangelicals, big corporations and the Republican Party' and law in the United States has become 'a tool of political warfare … freedom of speech is but a slogan of the American government and media since most privately owned media firms are wedded to capital and interest groups in connection with the pork-barrelling of both Democratic and Republican politicians'.[43]

These problems explain American disaffection with their democracy, China's argument concludes, because it excludes ordinary citizens, does not reflect their will, and explains the social and political upheaval evident in the profound divisions within the society.

China claims that, in contrast, its 'whole-process people's democracy' is a system which, flourishing in the 'national conditions' of Chinese society, is 'a true democracy that works'.[44] Government by the Communist Party ensures order, stability, and economic progress under its unified leadership, an efficient arrangement that has seen China make such strides that it has become the second-largest economy in the world – set to become *the* largest by 2050 – raising living standards for all, achieving 'freedom from want', and more than doubling life expectancy from thirty-five years in 1949 (the year in which the People's Republic of China was founded) to 77.3 years by 2019. Criticisms of one-party rule are misguided, China says, because there are indeed several parties in the state; the Communist Party is the governing party and the others are 'advisors and assistants' which accept its leadership, so the state has a 'multiparty cooperation system'.[45] The unity and progress achieved commands over ninety per cent approval from the Chinese people.[46] 'Beijing also argues that "One Person, One Vote is a democratic principle, but it is by no means the only principle, nor does it of itself create democracy". In this context, Chinese leaders are selected based on their moral qualities and competence rather than solely through popular vote'.[47] As China's State Council Information Office put it in 2021, 'Democracy and dictatorship appear to be a contradiction in terms, but together they ensure the people's status as masters of the country. A tiny minority is sanctioned in the interests of the great majority, and "dictatorship" serves democracy'.[48] This is justified by the claim that it is the people collectively who are the masters, and given that a collective requires a directing leadership, the CCP provides it – thus in effect reprising the Roman idea of 'dictatorship' by one who holds the power to say on the collective's behalf and in its interests what is to be done.[49] In the words of China's State Council Information Office, CCP 'leadership is the fundamental guarantee for whole-process people's democracy'.[50]

China argues that democracy has two levels: 'On a national level, it refers to the people's status as masters of their own country; on an international level, it refers to the democratic relations between nations'.[51] It charges the US with creating division and confrontation, forcing states to take sides, for the sake of its global control and material interests. This, says China, is evidenced by NATO, the 'Five Eyes' (the Anglosphere intelligence alliance comprising the US, the UK, Canada, Australia and New Zealand), the 'Quad' (Quadrilateral Security Dialogue comprising the US, India, Australia and Japan) and AUKUS (the trilateral defence and security pact of the US, the UK and Australia; Beijing describes the latter as a 'racist clique'). It is further evidenced by the Iraq and Afghanistan wars, demonstrating that:

what the United States really cares about are the so-called order and hierarchy in international relations to secure its hegemonic status. Once such a hierarchical concept is involved, there will be no real democracy. The US regards itself as a leader, and through long-arm jurisdiction, it abuses domestic laws and implements them in the international community, oppresses other countries at will, and seeks only its self-interest.[52]

By contrast, China asserts that it never seeks to interfere in the internal affairs of other countries, but strives to promote an international order premised on 'mutual respect, fairness and justice, and win-win cooperation'.[53]

In arguing that the international order should be a democracy, China is using the liberal concept of equality and justice – conceiving of states on the Westphalian model as equal self-determining partners – against itself to oppose the hegemonic system constructed by the US through its hierarchical alliances and patron–client relationships, with states dependent on it for security and aid. In a 2022 speech Xi Jinping placed stress on this point by iterating China's opposition to 'all forms of unilateralism and the forming of blocs and exclusive groups targeted against particular countries'.[54]

It has to be granted that China's criticism of the US's domestic politics is telling and hard to refute. Many of these criticisms apply to other Western states, especially those with plurality voting systems that drive two-party divisions that turn government into acrimonious party political battlegrounds, inflamed by the distorting influence of big money and the consequent inequalities and injustices that disaffect the populace. Likewise, China's characterisation of the US-constructed world order since 1945 is accurate, though it ignores the historical and geopolitical conditions that impelled the world into defensive and mutually hostile blocs, in significant part explained by the internal politics and external actions of the authoritarian states that initiated the tensions. Today's Western alliances were formed against Nazism and Japanese militarism, and remained in ever-more-consolidated place by the Soviet Union's capture of Eastern Europe and the attempted spread of its authoritarian ideology through 'Comintern' and subversion activities; while more latterly the ballooning power of China and its dominance in East and South Asia, to say nothing of its economic and ideological penetration of Africa and South America, keep the Western states in a posture of containment by means of the network of alliances and US military bases that respectively ring the Russian and Chinese spheres. Even the most cynical interpretation of the latter cannot construe containment as being at least in significant part reactive rather than merely aggressive.

But China's defence of its internal arrangements and its international behaviour do not survive a moment's examination. There is no rule of law in China in the core sense of government being answerable to law with an independent judiciary and an order of human rights and civil liberties that protect individuals from the power of the state. China's human rights record is appalling: open-ended 'administrative detention' and 'educational placements' without trial, slave-labour camps, oppression of Uyghurs and Tibetans, absence of rights to freedom of expression and assembly,[55] the death penalty for dozens of offences including not just murder, rape and 'subversion of the state' (widely defined to include dissent and opposition) but also embezzlement, corruption, bribery, insubordination in the armed forces – the list is long – are just a few examples of its repressive and coercive nature, making it a state in which people are not citizens but subjects under the powerful control of the CCP.[56] I acted for an NGO at the UN Human Rights Council in Geneva in the 1990s on China's human rights violations, at which time – shortly after the events of 4 June 1989 in Tiananmen Square – I also chaired a UK organisation for Chinese asylum applicants seeking refuge from persecution for their pro-democracy and labour rights activities in China.[57] First-hand accounts of victims make the suppression of Hong Kong democracy advocates (at this precise moment of writing dozens of such activists have been imprisoned there for opposition to increasingly draconian laws suppressing freedoms) more than just a news item.[58] In the 'patriot only' elections in Hong Kong in 2023 – 'patriot only' is a speaking categorisation; democracy parties were banned from participation – a legislature was formed that was tailored to Beijing's plans for suppressing the democracy movement and sending its proponents to jail.[59]

China's definition of its version of 'democracy' is most accurately described by the colloquial expression 'gaslighting', most especially directed at its own people, 'gaslighting' being psychological manipulation that distorts reality, distracts attention and plants beliefs that give the gaslighter control. The people of China have no say over CCP policy, are punished for disagreeing or failing to comply, are under constant and repressive surveillance and censorship – in short, are subject to the exercise of arbitrary rule without recourse. By contrast, in Western democracies civil liberties protected by the rule of law remain despite the increasing failure of governments to ensure a just distribution of social and economic goods – the situation exemplified by the vastly increasing wealth of a few while at the bottom of society indigents sleep on the streets. China's CCP offers material security in return for subjection, and many accept the trade-off – despite the fact that inequalities as great as in the West exist there, as can be seen when the Party elite and those who have benefitted from state-enabled commerce are contrasted with the general population: according to the Forbes 'rich list', in order to count among the top 100 Chinese billionaires an individual has to have a minimum net worth of $3.9 billion; the Hurun Rich List says there are 814 billionaires in China.[60]

It might be supposed that authoritarian politicians in the West think that the Chinese trade-off between prosperity and civil liberties will serve their own turn. But if the evidence of, for example, Venezuela is considered, the authoritarians' motivation might simply be gaining and retaining possession of power, requiring the forcible repression of opposition, whatever the consequences for the general populace. That was the situation in China until the end of the Cultural Revolution in the late 1970s, when the Party appears to have realised that their retention of power required pacifying the population through material benefits as well as repression.[61] The crop of authoritarians at time of writing, exemplified in this instance by Donald Trump, seem to have plutocrats rather than the general populace as proposed beneficiaries, not least because it is the latter who enable them into power and, for their own ends, wish to keep them there.[62]

The most valued features of Western-style liberal democracy are the rule of law and civil liberties. These are the central targets of attack by authoritarian movements, whether of left or right, whether from internal or external sources, whether deliberate and orchestrated as by Russia and China, or the spontaneous cumulative result of inflammatory online echo chambers propagating misinformation and division. The problem is clear; how to deal with it while preserving the best features of liberal democracy is vigorously under discussion. The next chapter discusses the remedy for liberal democracy's failure to deliver its promise as the result of its capture by factionalist politics and big money, these jointly constituting one of the chief threats to it – a threat it poses to itself all by itself. In the remainder of this chapter the subject is proposals to counter internal and external anti-democracy threats from authoritarianism, beginning with the problem of internet platforms.

The giant internet platforms of Meta, Amazon, Google, Apple and Twitter ('X') were already hugely rich and powerful by the time of the Covid-19 pandemic, and became even more so because of it. Lockdowns made reliance on their services spike yet further, and in the pandemic's wake a significant part of working life and consumer activity stayed online. While there were already questions about the platforms' monopolistic sway over large tracts of the economy, inviting consideration of antitrust and anti-monopoly responses, a still more pressing question relates to their control of information and how this affects politics. Anxieties are felt on both the (non-extremist) left and right of the political spectrum; in the US Democrats express concern about interference from domestic and foreign extremists, while Republicans claim that internet content is biased against conservative views.

Among the initiatives proposed are, variously or in combination, antitrust moves to break up the platforms, stricter regulation, and promotion of 'middleware' platforms designed to enable individuals to choose how they use the information they encounter.[63] The EU has chosen the antitrust route together with, in some member states, stricter regulation – Germany passed a Network Enforcement Act in 2017 aimed at curtailing hate speech, fake news and misinformation, imposing large fines (up to $50 million) if content specified as unacceptable is not removed within forty-eight hours of being detected.[64] Regulation invites challenges over freedom of expression, while antitrust legislation has long (though attitudes are changing) been regarded as punishing corporations for the success they achieved by the efficiencies of scale. In any case consumers highly value the tech giants' products and services, so the argument that their monopolistic character skews the market and adversely affects consumer welfare does not persuade.

But this is not the point; the point is that their control of information threatens democracy.

Since 2016, Americans have woken up to the power of technology companies to shape information. These platforms have allowed hoaxers to peddle fake news and extremists to push conspiracy theories. They have created 'filter bubbles,' an environment in which, because of how their algorithms work, users are exposed only to information that confirms their pre-existing beliefs. And they can amplify or bury particular voices, thus having a disturbing influence on democratic political debate. The ultimate fear is that the platforms have amassed so much power that they could sway an election, either deliberately or unwittingly.[65]

The authors of this remark, writing in 2020, went on to speculate:

Suppose that one of these giants were taken over by a conservative billionaire. Rupert Murdoch's control over Fox News and *The Wall Street Journal* already gives him far-reaching political clout, but at least the effects of that control are plain to see: you know when you are reading a *Wall Street Journal* editorial or watching Fox News. But if Murdoch were to control Facebook or Google, he could subtly alter ranking or search algorithms to shape what users see and read, potentially affecting their political views without their awareness or consent. And the platforms' dominance makes their influence hard to escape.[66]

Their prescience is commendable; Elon Musk bought Twitter in 2022, and supported Donald Trump in 2024.

As a result of uncertainty about how to proceed, the default has so far been to encourage the platform giants to self-regulate. That, predictably, has not worked – rather the opposite; witness Meta's abandonment of supervision of misinformation and hate speech posted on its platforms – and the threat posed by the information monopoly remains. The history of efforts in the US to legislate for balance and responsibility in news and media discussion of politics is one of failure; the fairness doctrine of the Federal Communications Commission was so strongly opposed by Republicans claiming bias against them that it was withdrawn as long ago as 1987.[67]

A different approach to the problem is offered by Francis Fukuyama and his co-authors with their suggestion of a 'middleware solution'.[68] 'Middleware' is software that overlays the content on an internet platform and modifies or comments upon it. Social media users could select a middleware service whose algorithms evaluate the significance and reliability of the data being presented. The concept is already familiar from one form of it, the function that enables one to block emails or messages from undesirable sources. Another example is how Wikipedia alerts a reader of one of its articles if evidence or a source is not cited for a claim made in it. The idea here is a more general version of such an intermediary. One can imagine a middleware which, when one encounters information on an internet platform, offers other sources of the same including critical or disagreeing content.

There is a strong case for the idea that all AI-generated content (essays written by ChatGPT for example) should be watermarked so that its provenance is clear. Unfortunately, technical dexterity by experts in the digital world means that such safeguards can be dodged. Middleware has the advantage that internet users can choose to apply it to sites and platforms, thus placing their content in better perspective.

Middleware platforms themselves would require to have neither too much nor too little power to come between the Big Tech platforms and consumers of their content, and the degree of power in question, together with the reliability and transparency of the providers, would need to be defined by law.[69] The idea has attractions, not least in not falling foul of freedom of expression anxieties; rather the contrary, for it offers the possibility of enacting the good idea that the way to deal with bad free speech is better free speech.[70]

Whatever solution is found to the problem of malevolent and subversive uses of the internet from agencies, witting or unwitting, seeking to overturn comities in which the rule of law and civil liberties are central, it needs to be found and implemented before the latter are lost. The idea that education can arm people against being misled is a noble one, and remains an aim to be pursued – this is the 'critical thinking' agenda in a nutshell – but it is far from a guarantee. Liberal democracy is a form of private enterprise, each individual with his or her own vote and the freedom to use it; but leaving its protection to the private enterprise of critical thinking has already proved to be ineffective. Middleware of the kind proposed might help, in equipping critical thinkers with more resources to think critically. But protecting liberal democracy is a community challenge, and fortunately while liberal democracy still exists the community can use its structures to do so.

Authoritarian challenges to liberal democracy operate on more fronts than the social media one, important though this is. One thoughtful response, in my view a highly valuable one, is offered by the 2023 report of the Committee on Political Affairs and Democracy to the Parliamentary Assembly of the Council of Europe.[71] Responding to 'the increase in recent years of far-right violence, driven by xenophobia, racism and other forms of intolerance, [and] the threats these actions pose to human rights, to the functioning of democratic institutions, and to diverse and inclusive societies', the report urges 'politicians and political parties' to be 'at the forefront of responses to far-right extremism, both in the public defence of human rights and democratic principles, and in the unequivocal rejection of all forms of racism and intolerance, hate speech, incitement to racial hatred and harassment.' It calls for a respectful and inclusive dialogue, and encourages political parties to sign the Charter of European political parties for a non-racist and inclusive society.[72] It is not irrelevant to mention that the rapporteur for the committee, Samad Seyidov of Azerbaijan, is a member of the European Conservatives Group and Democratic Alliance, a group in the Parliamentary Assembly of the Council of Europe.

The full text of the report appears as Appendix II. An explanatory background to the report's findings and recommendations is given by Seyidov in section 1 and its recommendations are listed in sections 14 and 15. These – indeed, all sections of the report – are essential reading.

INTERFERENCE UNDERMINING DEMOCRACY

In the decades after the mid-twentieth century, Western democracies – most notably the US – perceived the threat to the central values of their systems of civil liberties, judicial independence and free markets as coming from extreme left ideologies, in particular communism. By the end of the first quarter of the twenty-first century the same threat, apart from the 'free market' idea which big business wishes to extend further (ideally, for them, into making the whole of society into a libertarian market), is perceived to come from the extreme right. To put matters in this way is to signal two important connected points, one being the simplisticism embodied in labels, the other being the commonalities underlying any ideologies whose practical implementation requires suppressing civil liberties and judicial independence.

'Free market' pieties have had to be tempered by a forest of regulations against the exploitations that the profit motive is ever-ready to make if it can get away with it, but the failure of totally centralised economic control of the kind attempted by the Soviet Union and its satellites demonstrates that, subject to restraints on exploitation and chicanery, markets are a reasonable and rational way of getting products and services – from chewing gum to airplanes, from plumbing repairs to insurance – from those who offer them to those who want them, subject to protection of the latter from fraud, abuse, and malpractice by vendors (whether individual retailers or multinational corporations) of goods and services. Contention arises over fundamentals like education, health, welfare and security; in Europe there is a presumption that these are to be provided by the community as a whole through pooling of resources, because they are the basis of equality of opportunity and concern. In the US, by contrast, education, health and social security are regarded as goods that should be private, purchasable at the user's own expense; the impracticability of this results in a grudging provision of minimal offerings of them (Medicare; Medicaid; public schools, half of whose graduates have literacy levels below the age of eleven; welfare stamps), leaving – in highly expensive form – the better or best versions of them to be bought by whoever can afford them.

Both left and right authoritarianism cannot tolerate freedoms in expression, assembly, the media, the courts, personal autonomy, dissent or opposition. Since these are pillars of democracy, authoritarianism cannot tolerate democracy, unless the term is redefined to a pretended sense of it as in China, or manipulated and hollowed out as in Putin's Russia and Orbán's Hungary.

The Seyidov report recognises that left-wing extremism still exists, noting that Europol had listed '414 failed, foiled or completed attacks in European Union countries' in the period 2006–20 'inspired by extreme left-wing and anarchist ideology', but that right-wing extremism, with its 'particular historical legacy in Europe' (Fascism and Nazism), is 'the fastest-growing threat in many European countries'.[73] He gives a definition of the expression 'far-right extremism', all three of its components required for a movement to fall under the label: 'First, a belief in some form of natural inequality or hierarchy between peoples or groups of people, which may include nationalism, nativism, racism, xenophobia, antisemitism,

Islamophobia, and homophobia. Second, a belief in authoritarianism. Third, an implicit or explicit aim to destroy the democratic system'.[74] The 'extreme' Right has to be distinguished from the 'radical' Right; the latter operates 'within the democratic processes, accepting popular sovereignty and the minimal procedural rules of parliamentary democracy, are hostile to liberal democracy and criticise its crucial aspects, such as pluralism and minority rights, and publicly condemns the use of violence as an instrument of politics'.[75] By contrast, the extreme Right is prepared to use violent action – rioting and hate speech count as such – and whereas the radical Right tends to be organised into political parties, extreme Right actors range from states (e.g. Russia) and political parties (e.g. the AfD in Germany) to movements (such as Golden Dawn in Greece and white supremacists in the US) to ad hoc groups (e.g. the 6 January Capitol Hill rioters) and individual activists using social media platforms.[76]

With these clarifications in view, Seyidov proceeds to analyse what drives the extreme Right. There is a consensus that crises such as the global financial meltdown of 2008 and the policy decisions that followed it – including austerity measures and the dramatic widening of an already egregious rich–poor gap – a rise in migration caused by conflict and climate conditions in regions close to Europe, the Covid pandemic, and the return of war on the European continent, are jointly to blame, prompting right-wing extremists to offer 'simplistic and stereotyped solutions in response to the anxieties and uncertainties' thus caused.[77] But the problem has been exacerbated by deficits in democracies themselves:

'unresolved identity-related issues, systemic poor governance, and administrative dysfunction. This can be compounded by low trust in mainstream media, low media literacy, and a lack of critical and independent journalism which, combined, can amplify vulnerability to disinformation'.[78]

The challenge confronting Europe is not confined to Europe, Seyidov notes; all of North and South America, Indonesia, India and Oceania are at risk to as great a degree. This global spread has much to do – perhaps everything to do – with the 'online extremist environment'. It facilitates networking among far-right groups, recruitment, and dissemination of materials promoting the ideology and encouraging its associated behaviours. Recruitment includes leading people online from less to more extreme sites successively, taking a recruit deeper into self-reinforcing echo chambers step by step. Attempts to counter these activities are easily avoided by extremists switching to different platforms, or using deniable coded messaging under freedom of expression provisions. In this way extremist ideas infiltrate the mainstream.[79]

And it is this last point which is most pertinent to the argument here.

> It is crucial to position extremism as a threat to democracy itself. It is both a direct threat because it jeopardises the democratic constitutional order and freedoms, and an indirect threat because it can distort political life. In 2003, the Assembly warned against traditional political parties being potentially tempted to adopt the stance and the demagogic discourse specific to extremist parties in order to counter the increasing

electoral popularity of the latter. Also in 2010, the Assembly expressed concern about the non-negligible risk that mainstream political parties tend to rely on racist discourse in order to avoid losing part of their electorate.[80]

Note the dates at which these concerns were voiced; since the second of them, what was feared has actually happened. The election of Donald Trump in 2024 is the capstone on this – to time of writing anyway.

One of the principal democratic norms, repeatedly identified in these pages, is a legal order which is independent of politics and government, and under which all are treated alike. In authoritarian dispensations leaders are above the law; that is one of the defining features of such systems. The spectacular failure of the US judicial system to hold Donald Trump to account by treating him in the same way as any other convicted felon places him above the law in exactly the same way as any authoritarian ruler in any other place or time.[81] If proof were needed of the fragility of democratic ideals, this single instance would be it.

Responding to extremism's threat requires a range of endeavours, from strengthening the structures and practices of democracy itself – an inward-facing endeavour – to the outward-facing endeavour of countering the spread of extremist propaganda and its reliance on misinformation, distortion, tactics of disruption, creation of divisions, recruitment of followers, and promotion of hate speech and other forms of violence. The latter is to be done by political, legal and educational measures. The inward- and outward-facing activities jointly constitute 'defensive democracy'.[82] Balancing freedom of expression rights with legal measures against extremist online content is one challenge; banning political parties or organisations advocating extremist policies is another. In this connection Seyidov quotes the Venice Commission, which:

> recommended that 'the competence of state authorities to dissolve a political party or prohibit one from being formed should concern exceptional circumstances, must be narrowly tailored and should be applied only in extreme cases. Such a high level of protection is appropriate, given the fundamental role of political parties in the democratic process that also requires a stricter level of scrutiny in comparison with other associations than political parties'.[83]

Along with these structural and legal measures a third domain of activity invites attention, namely, education, both formal and more generally in the wakening of society to the threat and encouraging its engagement not only in opposition to extremism but in support of inclusion and pluralism. And finally – not least – the major underlying factors that provide extremism with its opportunity have to be addressed: economic inequality and social injustices.[84]

Whereas all these measures are necessary and connected, central to them is getting the structures and processes of democracy itself right. The other measures require that they work well, because it is precisely their ceasing to do so that has created the opportunity for extremism. The structures and processes of democracy that evolved from the end of the eighteenth century until the years immediately after the Second World War served adequately enough, and shepherded many benefits into existence as a result; but as franchises extended and populations grew, the initial forms first began to creak under the pressure, and in the course of the last couple of decades before this writing have bent out of shape entirely.

The problem is not irremediable, far from it; but remedying it is essential – and urgent. How to do this is the subject of the next chapter.

5

RESTORING DEMOCRACY

In the Introduction the reasons for the current faltering condition of democracy were listed:

- It is not delivering enough for people's aspirations and needs.
- The power of high finance is distorting it.
- Authoritarian models of government are attracting attention as alternatives.
- There are both orchestrated and un-orchestrated attacks on democracy from internal and external forces, acting in the interest of the authoritarian model.

The reasons are connected. In chapter 1 an account is given of the way *party politics* has usurped government – a distortion compounded by the capture of party politics by big money, plus the inability of national governments to control multinational business, this latter point discussed in chapter 2. The result has been the alienation of populaces from democracy because of the inequalities and injustices that arise from partisan political government and the influence of those with the financial power to bend it to their interests. Authoritarian political movements in Western countries use the disaffection thus aroused to seek power – not to solve the problem of those inequalities and injustices, but instead to entrench partisan political power further, namely, *their* brand of partisan politics, together with the interests of big money that support them. This is the toxic contradiction of populism, discussed in chapter 3: it is not about 'the people' but even more emphatically about partisan politicians and the interests that support them. The means employed by authoritarians – today, the political far right; but both extremes of politics on left and right come to the same thing – to destabilise democracy are various; in addition to capitalising on popular discontents over immigration and blaming 'elites' and current political establishments (this latter point too well justified), they conduct overt and covert attacks on democratic ideals through the methods and means, not the least among the latter social media, discussed in chapter 4.

In the Introduction it was also made clear why protecting democracy, understood in the most general sense, is vitally important: it is because democracy embodies civil liberties, human rights, and a rule of law that respects and when relevant protects those rights and liberties. Authoritarian regimes are defined precisely by their disregard of liberties and rights and their usurpation of the rule of law. The battle lines could not be more sharply and clearly drawn. In a democracy you can read a book of this type; in an authoritarian state you might and probably would be forbidden to do so, in which case its writer and reader might find themselves in the same prison for the former having written it and the latter having read it. Such a state of affairs is an attack on the human spirit itself.

This is why democracy must be defended. In this chapter, proposals for defending – restoring, rehabilitating – democracy are offered.

One thing to mention straight away is that in saying that *party political capture of government* is to blame, one is *not* saying that *there should not be politics or political parties*. Political debate is about choices and direction of travel; political parties are organisations that formulate and offer proposals about these matters; both are vital in a democracy, where the rights of freedom of expression, opinion and assembly, and the consent of the populace to how their country is run, are central elements of the liberties and rights that define it. The formation of government requires debate about public policy possibilities and alternatives, indeed demands that these should be explored and analysed, criticised and defended, explained and judged, in the processes through which government is set up.

But – and this is *the* big But – in the nature of democracy as it has evolved to its present condition, *especially* in first-past-the-post ('plurality') electoral systems, what happens is that once a government is formed it acts as if its side of these debates had won outright, as if other points of view had not been put forward at all and did not matter. This is the sense in which *partisan political government* – 'factionalism' in James Madison's sense – has evolved as a result of political parties becoming authoritarian structures themselves, in which career politicians have to obey a party line in order to retain and advance their careers, making them vulnerable to influence both from party discipline and, as individuals and for their party, from donors, lobbyists and vested interests working to get advantage by having the party they supported into government legislate and otherwise act on their behalf.

The ideal of a legislature composed of independent members who examine policy on its merits such that the case for it has to persuade if it is to pass, rather than being automatically voted through on the instructions of a party leadership whatever any individual member thinks, is doubtless just that: an ideal. But in a proportional electoral system the diversity of the legislature's membership will take government far closer to this ideal than a single party in control of the legislature and therefore acting, between elections, as if they governed a one-party state. That is *de facto* how government works in winner-takes-all (meaning: all power) plurality systems. And that is the key source of the problems that now make democracy vulnerable, given that major examples of winner-takes-all democracies – the US, the UK, India, Canada and several dozen more – operate on this basis.[1]

Another thing to mention straight away is an important reminder about civil liberties, human rights and the rule of law. This is that these were hard-won, very hard-won, over an extended period of centuries in which many suffered to achieve them. I recount this in my *Towards the Light*,[2] summarising its point thus: the rights and liberties possessed by all citizens in a democracy today were once the possession of extremely few: only royalty, aristocrats, church dignitaries and the wealthy – if these latter were different from the first three categories, which generally they were not – enjoyed satisfactory measures of freedoms and goods ('goods' including education, freedom to travel, immunities from restrictions that applied to the majority, and generally healthy living conditions such as good diet and housing), while by contrast peasants, serfs, slaves, workers, women, indeed most of the general populace, lived at or close to subsistence levels, the great majority of them illiterate, most of them confined to a few square kilometres they never left between birth and an early grave, where they worked on the land, at a trade or in domestic servitude, generally under obedience to a master above them in a hierarchy. They had no say; they had only the imperative to obey and endure. The extent of their personal competence was severely limited, even in many cases as regards whom they could marry, where they could live, what they were allowed to believe. Apart from a few failed attempts at rebellion in the high medieval and Renaissance periods, the generality of the populace lived voiceless and highly constrained lives.

From the seventeenth century onwards the struggle to break the bonds of this condition, enabled by the spread of globalisation and changing economic conditions with their attendant social developments, began to achieve successes. A middle class grew in size and wealth, and wanted more say; and got it. The movements that secured the vote, labour rights, emancipation from slavery, women's rights, more just laws and general education, thus spreading this achievement more widely, gained their successes in halting and variably paced ways through the eighteenth and nineteenth centuries and into the twentieth. Many of those who fought for these things did not live to see them materialise because the effort took longer than normal human lifespans. The struggle to achieve them was hard indeed; possessors of power are reluctant to yield it. Their fingers had to be prised from it one by one with great and courageous strength. Most of us in Western democracies take these achievements for granted now, alas, unaware of how vulnerable they are to overthrow by authoritarianism. The very openness and tolerance of democratic civil liberties allows the intolerant and authoritarian to insert their views and use the institutions that embody these liberties to get into a position to negate them – an example is the 'one last democratic vote' phenomenon, a vote cast for a populist party that puts an end to elections when in power, as happened in Nazi Germany and as has happened too often elsewhere.

It was the eighteenth-century Enlightenment that most clearly articulated, and most successfully won, the argument for rights, liberties and the rule of law. The history of Western polities since the late eighteenth century is in large part a history of these concepts being increasingly applied in practice, taking concrete form; although it is also the history of efforts by counter-Enlightenment forces to combat them and re-establish in modern versions – even to the extent of waging war – the control formerly exercised by absolute monarchs and an all-powerful church. What authoritarianism thus offers is a return, in its effect, to conditions of a kind of serfdom for most. The serfdom of the Chinese under the CCP is sweetened by improved living standards and access to a consumer lifestyle, but in respect of liberties and rights it is serfdom nonetheless. The serfdom of Venezuelans under Maduro makes people suffer the loss of rights without compensatory consumerism and its living standards. In a contest between the desire to have and maintain power, on the one hand, and the welfare of the people, on the other, the former will always win – even in a Western liberal democracy.

In its most general sense the term 'liberal' applies to dispensations where the rights and liberties constitutive of democracy apply – hence the term 'liberal democracy' itself, which is in fact a pleonasm: the two words in the phrase are practically synonyms. 'Liberalism' as a theoretical term in political philosophy and practical politics has come to mean a number of varying things to different people, but the foundational idea at work is the 'small-l' liberal idea of an open, inclusive, pluralist, rights-based order. For those on the further reaches of the left and right the term has come to be a term of contempt. For the further left it is wishy-washy, too concessive to capitalism, too accommodating to disparities in society; to the further right it gives too much say and too many inconvenient protections to everyone, obstructing what authoritarians wish to do and have. Both extremes wish to get rid of it, and one line of attack on it is to portray it as old-fashioned, passé, unfit.

This is a serious mistake. Compare the social and political gains of the last few centuries in the West with the gains made by scientific enquiry. We do not regard scientific advances made in the past as boring and old-fashioned just because they were made in the past, but retain those that work, and build on others to discover more. Some earlier scientific results are a permanent possession of humanity's self-education, and many others provide the basis of further and more inclusive developments; the classical physics initiated by Galileo and Newton still apply as approximations at modest scales of velocity and energy, and count as a special case of modern physics. Although politics can bend some of science to bad ends – nuclear weapons provide a salient example – medical technologies, computers, electric light, and so much more, are things we would not be without. Likewise the gains of social and political thinking – the application of ideas about rights, liberties and the rule of law – are permanent possessions of the human story, serving as the basis for development of good societies in which good individual lives can be possible. Reflect on the fact that good individual lives require the right to choose and to have a say, a generous degree of autonomy, protection from being preyed upon, exploited and abused, and the rest of what lists of civil liberties and human rights specify; these are the necessary conditions for 'a good life' to be possible for every individual to exercise his or her capacities in pursuit of realising his or her conception of a life that is good to live.

These rights and liberties are inconvenient to those who wish to aggregate power to themselves, 'power' not just in the sense of ruling over others, but in what high degrees of wealth and privilege give access to – namely, a jump to a position at the head of every queue, having the best of what is available in life, rising above the constraints that apply to the majority – constraints which allow the powerful few to have their own way because they keep the majority out of their path. In principle there is nothing wrong with anyone being rich providing it is not at the expense of others being poor; but the fact that some live in conspicuous luxury while others sleep on the streets and search for food in rubbish bins is proof that the arrangements favour the former, channelling wealth and its power to them to ensure that the system works to their advantage.

Distorting the system in favour of those who have the means to distort it has been a perennial in human affairs, and democracy – the system that aims to share rights and liberties and give everyone a say – is the great idea that the struggles of the last few centuries have sought to actualise. The struggles made much progress – but incompletely, and now opposition to them is pushing back against that progress, seeking to reverse it and to restore how things were before the struggles started taking effect.

So: defending democracy is a vital and urgent task. The first step in doing so is to make luminously clear this point: that *the purpose of democratic government is to serve the best interests of all.* 'The people' in a democracy are the '*of* the people' people: everyone. Not just the voters who supported a given party, not just business, not just vested interests which helped a political party gain power. These latter have become the '*for* the people' people. Nor is it the purpose of government to hold and pull the levers of state power in service to an ideological programme which it is determined to impose on everyone whether or not they agree. Instead, the purpose of government is to manage the society and economy in optimal ways for all on their behalf, guided by the best route through the diversity of needs, interests and desires that exist in a society, which consist of a patchwork of individuals and minorities – recall the point made in chapter 1 that there are few if any 'natural majorities' for anything in society except artificially at election or referendum moments, because society is a congeries of individuals and minorities which sometimes overlap and sometimes diverge in their needs, interests and desires.

In thus identifying the *purpose* of government, one is making an *ethical* point: a point about the character, the nature, of government; what it is for is defined by what it exists to serve, and what it exists to serve can be summarised as the welfare of the people in the state they constitute, given that the people want to fare well, and they bestow authority on government precisely on the understanding that it will act to that end. The state is not an entity separable from its populace, though typically governments act as if it were; policies relating to foreign affairs, defence and the economy have been in the past, and still are today, standardly implemented irrespective of their effect on whole sections of society. A salient example is the waging of war, especially war which is not purely defensive. Nor is government an entity separable from the people, though once again government *qua* party political government behaves as if it were because of the political imperatives involved in maintaining its hold on power.

Obviously, the cliché 'you can't please everyone all the time' (most clichés are true) applies. Choices have to be made that will be preferred more by some than others, though choices that actively disadvantage some in order to advantage others are intrinsically suspect and, if such have to be made, require a watertight justification. But certain generalisations apply that are indeed in the interests of everyone and, in light of the purpose of democratic government, they are non-negotiable. One is that upholding the rights and liberties of every individual is in all individuals' interests. Another is that upholding the rule of law without fear or favour is in everyone's interests, not just those of individuals but of business and civil society alike, because it exists to respect and when relevant protect rights and liberties.

A third is that maximising social justice, ensuring that the opportunity playing field is as level as possible through giving everyone their best chances by equal access to education, healthcare, and a say, is a necessity for promoting and protecting those rights and liberties.

A fourth is that a civilised society is marked as such by its treatment of the weakest, the poorest, the sick and the incapacitated, and all those least able to manage the complexities of modern society or disadvantaged by them. This means that through pooling resources the society, through the service of government, cares for its own, and does so decently, not grudgingly or scrimpingly.

Note that this list of generalisations fades as it lengthens in the actual practice of democracies as they currently exist. The first two are reasonably well applied on the whole – so far – while the third and fourth are not. The US, for example, fails miserably on the third and fourth. It does not do well on the second either; the rich and powerful are treated differently before the law, as egregiously exemplified by the case of Donald Trump who turns out to have been as far above the law as Ivan the Terrible or Genghis Khan. These are hollowing-outs of a democratic order, and a bad sign. They indicate that government is too much the plaything of politicians, not a service to all the people; it indicates that the purpose for which it exists is subverted by partisan interests.

The question therefore becomes: how can government be constructed so that it serves the purpose that it is meant to serve in a democracy? The answer is: by a constitution that explicitly directs the activities of government – which means the offices of government and all those elected or appointed to occupy them – to the express fulfilment of that purpose. For brevity let us call this the *constitutional imperative*. Despite both the simplicity of its appearance, and the vague thought that this is anyway what constitutions, whether codified or not, are supposed to do, the idea of a constitutional imperative is pregnant with significance and requires explication.

Consider why a constitution is necessary. In a democracy a government has to be formed with and by the consent of the people, 'people' here denoting those enfranchised. The first thing to insist upon is that the franchise must be as wide and inclusive as possible, and that each vote must be equal to all others in its effect on the outcome; and that means that the electoral system must be proportional. It also means that the hidden Big Vote of money must be taken out of the process, as one of the chief means of distorting it.

To get from what the voters say to a government that serves them requires that there be institutions – executive, legislature, a judiciary, security agencies – that in their very construction act always to put the purpose of government into effect. This is a vital point: the *institutions* have to be such as to prevent those who are elected or appointed to them from acting outside the powers that the institutions are set up to exercise, but always in conformity with the express reason for which they exist.

The second thing to insist upon is that because in populous nations the democracy has to be republican, that is, exercised through representation, the 'consent of the people' has to be understood literally. Representatives are not delegates merely reporting some numinous abstraction called 'the will of the people', but individuals tasked with acting on the people's behalf, of course bearing their 'will' (their desires, interests and needs) very much in mind, but working out how it can be optimally served in light of the diversity of willings in the population (not just the electorate) as a whole – which often enough means identifying the best interests of the people collectively, with the consequence that the will of some of the people might not be enacted. By participating in the process of selecting representatives, the people recognise, explicitly, that what they endow them with is consent to act on their behalf, not an instruction merely to pass on their wishes. If the people do not like the way their representatives act on their behalf, they can throw them out by a due process, and choose others in their place. Representatives are tasked with getting information, listening to debate, analysing and evaluating policy proposals, and forming judgements on the best course to serve the people's good. Their own personal interests and careers are not one whit the point. We expect doctors and lawyers, teachers and electricians, to act thus – to act professionally; all the more should representatives of the people do so, because the stakes are as high or higher, and far more general.

In the ideal, voters would be well-informed and careful in their choice of representatives. But this cannot be taken for granted, not least because the party political system effectively imposes an at least very limited choice of candidates on electors, who anyway tend to decide by party label rather than individual merit. Moreover the small number of parties – in a plurality system only two have a real chance of forming a government – means that electors get a very restricted menu of policy and personnel options to choose from. Their choice is therefore not much of a choice at all; for over half of voters in a plurality system it is typically a Hobson's Choice, one in reality already made for them. In a proportional system the merits of candidates and policy options count for considerably more.

In another ideal, people who offer themselves for service in any of the branches of government, and especially those who might seek to legislate and/or direct offices of state, should be people of integrity, intelligence, common sense, altruism and experience, committed not to their own good but the people's good. No doubt some are; no doubt quite a few start out intending to be so; and history offers examples of statesmen and -women who have done noble things. Both history and contemporary times offer even more examples of people who are decidedly not statespersons or people of integrity. 'Career politicians' and 'machine politicians', for whom principle melts before expedience as rapidly and completely as snow in summer, are too common.[3]

Because there cannot be reliance on either the electorate or politicians being ideal in the required ways – no disparagement is intended to the people; this is just the voice of practicality, heard from Plato to James Madison and into our own times – the institutions of government have to be such that the right of the people to their say connects effectively with a second right they have, viz. *the right to good government* (to 'good enough' government, as the realist and man of common sense Aristotle put it). This is where the design of institutions comes in – and this, in the end, is *the* key consideration. It reprises the point made long ago by Livy in his History of Rome, *Ab Urbe Condita*, where he says at the beginning of Book II that when the Romans kicked out the last of their kings they put *the rule of law* in place of *rule by men* – meaning, institutions organised to ensure that the arbitrariness of personal interests, power-hunger and whim are not in charge. Of course, agreement on the design of institutions requires that the people are at their best when constructing them; the reassuring thought in this connection is that mere self-interest can induce careful thought, for people need only reflect on how they might be affected if a party they dislike gets into government and uses the overweening power at its disposal.

Whatever the detailed provisions look like in the design of institutions, the general requirement is that they should specify adherence to the purpose of government; should define the duties, powers, and limitations on powers, of elected and appointed office holders in order to direct them to service of that purpose; and should provide effective remedies against failure to observe these requirements in any way. This states the fundamental principle upon which a constitution should rest. In the US it is both a piety and yet in many cases a practical benefit that the Constitution's provisions must be observed, and invocation of them settles matters. There are – see below – some unsatisfactory things about the US Constitution, but in the generality of its effect it is a model of what a constitution should do.

Government has to have some discretionary powers to deal with untoward circumstances. Assumption of these powers has to be extremely well justified, and explicitly time-limited. Even if emergency powers are required for an extended period, as for example wartime, they should have to be periodically renewed with the same level of justification given. For control of the assumption and exercise of discretionary powers, a constitutional court or at least an independent judiciary with powers of review over government action is a necessity. There has to be extraordinary judicial competence for extraordinary circumstances, sufficient to order a general election or in very extreme cases to order the suspension of an officer of state. A system without checks of these ultimate kinds remains susceptible to abuse. Abuse might also occur if the constitutional court and judiciary are not themselves unimpeachably appointed, and required by the terms of their office to act with great caution and justification when circumstances are fraught.

And finally: the constitution has to be clearly set out and its terms known to all. This requires codification, and its dissemination through mandatory formal and informal education. Circumstances change, and history moves on; a constitution has to evolve accordingly; not in knee-jerk response to fashion or crisis, but flexibly and with sensible diligence. It must therefore provide for its own evolution through mechanisms that are agreed and clear. One of the faults of the US Constitution is its inertia in this respect; having assumed the status of holy writ, amending it takes a mountainous effort. As already mentioned, the point about the 'right to bear arms' is an especially sore example: when the right was accorded in the Second Amendment, adopted in 1791, 'arms' were muzzle-loading muskets – single-shot, short-range and very inaccurate; today they are powerful automatic assault weapons and even rocket-launchers. It is a signal of a kind of madness that the National Rifle Association and the gun lobby generally can keep in being, indeed progressively inflame, a murderously dangerous situation by invoking the Amendment as if it had the irresistible authority of scripture.

The foregoing is a sketch of constitutional principle. Codification, clarity and sensible reflective flexibility over time are its necessary features, but the most important thing is its point: to define and assert the purpose of government, and to ensure that government serves that purpose. Its allocation of duties and powers to the organs and officers of government must explicitly be directed at fulfilling that purpose, and that purpose, to repeat yet again, is: serving the interests of the people. This is the constitutional imperative. It can be described equally well by saying that government is the servant of the people, not their master. Democracy should not produce dictators; its very essence is meant to be protection against that outcome. That authoritarianism has taken rise from perversions of democracy in Turkey, Hungary, certain Central Asian states, to say nothing of the Russia bequeathed by Yeltsin to Putin and now – alarmingly – the US itself, is an illustration of the danger that democracy faces everywhere.

Grant that nothing can ever be perfect in human affairs, but note that it is not outwith human intelligence and goodwill to strive to optimise them, and actually to achieve optimality. For a democracy to be optimal, good voters and good politicians are necessary; but most necessary of all are good institutions to provide a steadying framework to account for the lapses and frailties of human nature. That is what a well-framed and well-aimed constitution offers.

A constitution is in essence no different in purpose from the rules of a club as these set out how the club is run. There are other rules a club will adopt, for example relating to the behaviour and dress code of members, which can be considered as analogous to the laws of a state; but the *constitutive* part of the rules apply to the club's governance – the structure of the managing committee, how they are elected or appointed, what their duties and responsibilities are, how they conduct the committee's business, how the club's finances are supervised, and what the members' rights and responsibilities are relative to the club's activities.

The rules of a club that deal with constitutive matters define the purposes for which the club exists, and the structures and conduct of the club's governance. Most constitutions of states deal explicitly with the second of these aspects, and only implicitly with the first; the question of why the state exists at all is merely assumed; and yet it is the most important matter, and explains why the second aspect has to be as it is. Historically, states existed primarily to protect and bolster the privileges of the ruling person or group within them. Doing so might have required the ruling elite – whether a monarch, big business and the political party they support, or a revolutionary 'vanguard' – to manage matters in such a way that the populations over which they ruled were productive enough and docile enough to provide what the ruling elite needed. The Enlightenment project was a rejection of this situation, seeking explicitly to replace it with the interests of the people *qua* individuals as the objective. Authoritarianism is about reversing that project. To prevent anyone or any group achieving this reversal, the structure and organisation of the state has to embody the objective of the people's interests, in particular by ensuring that the general interest cannot be subordinated to partisan interests, which includes any that claim (as the CCP does) to be the interpreter and custodian of the people's interests. Indeed, all political parties everywhere lay claim to knowing and having at heart the people's best interests. A test of whether this is so is whether an explicit or implicit 'even if' clause is lodged in the would-be ruler's claim to power: 'even if some of the population has to accept or suffer the imposition of disadvantage so that others can benefit ... even if certain rights have to be forgone ... even if those in power are not subject to the same laws as the rest ...' are prime examples.

'The interests of the people' are not hard to identify. They are the interests of each individual person. They are made explicit in every human rights declaration and instrument. They are for equality under the law, and a genuinely fair opportunity to make a life in society and to benefit from the goods of participation in it. These constitute a minimum. Access to good health and education services, and an equally effective voice in choosing the government under which a person will live, are constitutive of fair opportunity. What individuals do with their opportunities is up to them; the energetic will flourish more than the lazy. Much more can and should be said about how to so optimise a good society as to optimise the chance of good individual lives within it, but the fundamentals of civil liberties, rights, and a rule of dispassionate and independent law securing them, are non-negotiable.

Focusing on the purpose of government as the starting point for identifying how government should be constituted has implicitly answered a question that anarchists will think has been begged. Anarchist challenges are directed against both the first and second aspects of why any club has rules. Anarchism is the view that states and governments by their nature violate the natural freedom of human beings; as the Russian anarchist Mikhail Bakunin (1814–76) put it, 'If there is a State, there must be domination of one class by another and, as a result, slavery; the State without slavery is unthinkable – and this is why we [anarchists] are the enemies of the State.'[4] Anarchists cite the state's monopoly of coercive power through law and the police, and by implication its use to privilege some over the rest. On this latter, too often, they have a point, especially in authoritarian dispensations. But the short answer to anarchism is that it is a bad idea because it is nothing more than libertarianism gone wild, licensing the strong to oppress the weak, removing protections from citizens, turning what should be a level playing field into a mountain peak occupied by the muscular few with, far below, a swampy plain where the rest flounder. Far right-wing politics is the worst of what a combination of anarchism and authoritarianism produces: control and restriction by the state of the generality of the populace, while reserving anarchy to the rich and powerful at the top – a ghastly hybrid.

This is the reason for saying that the purpose of government is an ethical matter: it is about the good of all by ensuring the best for each, effected by just and rational means based on the liberties and rights of each and a level playing field for individuals to make use of them.

A different challenge will come from those who think that the GDP of the state and the profits of its enterprises matter so much that inequitable distributions are justified – for example, as a result of tax regimes that incentivise wealth-makers and thereby increase the amount of money available to the state. This assumes that there is an inevitable trade-off between social justice and national wealth, the cost of the first weighing too heavily on creation of the second: a zero-sum game. There are several replies to this. One is to argue that GNH (gross national happiness) is more important than GDP, and that GNH is increased by social justice and less consumerism. Another is to argue that a happier society can be a more productive one; if all employees had stakes in enterprises and shared their profits, this might be an expected result. A third is to point out that today's billionaires, if taxed proportionally (without tax havens and tricksy tax avoidance opportunities bought by their wealth), would still be very rich while making a greater return to society from their success. These are mere sketches of answers, and yes: money matters, but it cannot matter more than justice. In today's US, UK and too many other democracies, money does matter more than justice. This imbalance lies at the root of their current problem.

To recapitulate so far: the principal features of the constitution of a state concern how government is formed and how it is run. The first is about the institutions of government: what they are, how they are staffed by election and appointment, and how they relate to each other. The second is about the operation of government: the relations between its institutions and the people. This second feature is where the crucial and fundamental issue lies, viz. the purpose of government: to serve the interests of the people. As Western democracies have evolved so far, it is uncomfortably as if government – party political government – has become like authoritarian government, in which it is not the government that serves the people but the people who serve the government, which of course means: the governors themselves.

Nevertheless: however excellently a constitution is framed, it cannot be proof against determined manipulators unless other matters are addressed. The Constitution of North Korea accords all sorts of rights and liberties to the citizens of that benighted place which they never for a moment enjoy. It is one thing to write a document full of fine words; it is another to address the context in which they can take effect.

It is assumed that an audit of government performance is carried out by voters at election times, and at all times by the media as 'the third estate' scrutinising politics and government. This audit by voters and the media is one of the chief ways of 'holding power to account'. To a degree this actually happens when the people reject a governing party if dissatisfied with it. The media, ever confusing 'the public interest' with 'what interests the public' and looking for opportunities to stir controversy to benefit their reader or viewer numbers, also manage to perform their third-estate obligations at times – at least as regards governments they dislike. As regards parties they support, their partisanship can be extreme; the Murdoch press is an example of a pollutant in the public debate, barely disguising bias under a pretence of scrutiny.

To support the constitution there have to be laws and practices that regulate the presence of big money in politics, that apply the same legal requirements and codes to members of legislatures and government executives as operate everywhere else in society, and which combat misinformation and deliberate bias in the media.

The first of these requires limits on the amount of money any one person or body can donate for political purposes, together with complete transparency about the source and amount of any such donation. One of the worst things to happen in the US in recent years is the 2010 Supreme Court decision in *Citizens United v. Federal Electoral Commission* that lifted restrictions on how much money can be donated to a politician, political party or political cause. As the Brennan Center for Justice puts it, 'While wealthy donors, corporations, and special interest groups have long had an outsized influence in elections, that sway has dramatically expanded since the *Citizens United* decision, with negative repercussions for American democracy and the fight against political corruption.'[5]

The second point about the legal provisions and codes that apply to legislators and government executives might surprise some readers. In any corporation it is illegal to bully or bribe an employee; in the UK Parliament bullying, bribery and blackmail are standard and accepted under the guise of the Whips' exercise of party discipline to keep MPs in line.[6] There is a Code of Conduct for MPs which requires that they tell the truth and that they act in the interests of the people and not themselves or their party when the people's interests do not coincide with these latter; the disparity between the Code and actual practice is so great as to be comical.

Careerism in politics is the portal through which these sins enter. One remedy is to separate the legislature and executive completely; in all Westminster model democracies other than the US the executive is drawn from the majority in the legislature, which makes the latter the creature of the former, and its members – anxious to get into the executive – obedient to party demands in order to keep their sheets clean. If the chief executive (President or Prime Minister) is elected separately from members of the legislature, and appoints an executive of appropriate expertise and talent, with the executive being answerable to the legislature, whose members (as in the US

FOR THE PEOPLE

and France) cannot be members of the executive while sitting in the legislature, at least one of the major Westminster model problems is obviated. Allowing members of the legislature to sit for one or a limited number of terms only, and/or populating the legislature by sortition, are other remedies.

The third point, about the media – online, print or broadcast – is essential for an informed and responsible debate in society about matters of public policy, and indeed all other matters of public concern. The media should of course be free, so 'prior restraint' is not acceptable; that is merely censorship, another typical mark of authoritarian arrangements. But irresponsible, misleading, violently partisan media should be held accountable for polluting the public conversation by strong *post facto* penalties. Germany has taken determined steps in this direction, and France likewise, while respecting the importance of freedom of expression: as one report of the German approach puts it:

> Germany has been eminent in the number and quality of legal and social initiatives against disinformation. The amendment to the Interstate Media Treaty (*Medienstaatsvertrag*) added measures to fight against disinformation and misinformation. The state media authorities have received competence to initiate proceedings against media outlets if the journalistic due diligence obligations have not been adequately respected.[7]

This is a measure one would like to see applied everywhere.

It seems to me, as an outside observer of the Scandinavian democracies, that the joint effect of their population size and their proportional electoral systems yields an optimal form of republican democracy – 'optimal' because, again accepting that nothing can be perfect in human affairs, they are in their way the best examples of what the democratic ideal can be. They lie at the sweet spot between the dysfunctional sprawling arrangements of the US and the mythological arrangements of the UK, on one hand, and on the other hand the attempt at more direct democracy in the Swiss referendum system, which latter generates – automatically, it seems – a persistently conservative and rather static political order. In the Swiss system population size is also a factor in its success as a country; taking it and the Scandinavian countries together suggests that the closer democratic institutions are to the people, the better they function.

This implies that in a large-population country – any country with a population in excess of, say, twenty-five million would for these purposes count as such – devolution is desirable, with regions having a degree of autonomy within the federated arrangements that allow for more responsive government. This contention might not immediately seem to be supported by examples of structurally federal states like the US, India, Germany, Canada and Australia – and certainly not the UK, where central government is highly dominant over the devolved regions – but insofar as they do not, it is because their kind and degree of devolved autonomy is open to question. That is a discussion for another place, mentioned in passing here only to acknowledge the tension between the population-size point and the practical effect of devolution in those countries. But the example of Scandinavia is too striking to ignore, and suggests that such a discussion would eminently be worth having.

Among the gains of a proportional electoral system are greater participation by voters and greater sensitivity to the texture of society in the agencies of government, because compromise and power-sharing is inevitable, the debates about policy are closer to home, and the objective of fulfilling the purpose of government more immediately attainable. Above all, achieving in its fullest sense the constitutional imperative of protecting individual rights and liberties carries an enormous promise: the realisation of greater social justice and with it greater social harmony.

There is an important idea involved in this last point: that a system which reflects and thereby respects the diversities in state and society sees *harmony* not *identity* as the route to flourishing. Nationalistic states, too often tending towards authoritarian characteristics when nationalism provokes xenophobia and its yet-worse cousin racism, by their very nature emphasise identity, and this can and often does in turn provoke identity-wars between different sections within the society.[8] When the rights and liberties of each citizen are given equal weight and equal protection, no citizen or community of them can be subjected to putatively superior claims for consideration by other citizens or communities. The great gain of true democracy – one in which representation and the constitutional imperative are well exemplified in the ways described in these pages – lies here. To save democracy, which means saving the rights, liberties and rule of law that even our imperfect current democracies embody, we have to restore it in the direction of this true version of itself. That is one of the most urgent tasks of our time.

***

To restate and summarise the points in this chapter together with those in the previous chapter about the corrosive influence of malign interferences: what is needed is a constitution which is clear and known to all, which specifies that the purpose of government is to serve the interests of *all* the people, and which accordingly defines the duties and extent of powers of its offices and officers, together with remedies against failure or abuse. The constitution has to be subject to a careful and judicious flexibility, ensured by a process itself constitutional, when significant changes in society, economy, technology and world affairs render its provisions in need of adaptation. A Bill of Rights that enshrines the principles basic to all human rights instruments has to be a central pillar of the constitution, because it is the rights and interests of the people – each of them individually – that democracy exists to serve.

The role of money in political parties and elections must be strictly limited. Elections have to be conducted on a proportional representation system that promotes multiparty political diversity in the legislature ('multiparty' meaning – desirably – greater than two-party: but how many parties achieve representation is a matter for voters). *Post facto* action against misinformation, disinformation and falsehood in all media must be taken. A desideratum that recommends itself is that independent but regulated anti-misinformation 'middleware' facilities should be widely available and promoted – some might even say that this should be a condition of allowing internet platforms such as Meta and X to operate; but beware creating instruments that can themselves be abused; it has to be done well. In general the proposals outlined in Appendix II are highly pertinent in this connection.

Judicial appointments have to be non-political and effected by a transparent and scrupulous process based on the provable fitness of appointees. No one, absolutely no one, should be above the law, which should be equally applicable to all. One of the most dismaying events of recent US history is that Trump, a convicted felon, simply escaped an application of the law that no one else would have escaped, because he is who he is. That is a corruption of the rule of law, and shocking to behold.

Civic education about the constitution, both formally and informally, should include an iterated emphasis on the personal duty of citizens to examine the fitness of election candidates and to be informed about current affairs and their implications. Proportional electoral systems are more likely to foster engagement of this kind in contrast to plurality systems, which alienate too many from the process of choosing who will populate the offices of government and monitoring how they perform in them.

These measures speak to what can be done within a state to protect and foster democracy. Although a state can act against the more malign effects of multinational business activities within its own borders, including holding companies to account for human and environmental abuses beyond its borders – some provisions of this kind already exist in some places – it requires international cooperation to restrain the negative aspects of multinational business, and in particular to end the currently legal robber-baron system of 'offshoring' trillions of dollars of wealth, depriving governments of revenue by escaping the responsibility of contributing, as the rest of the country's employed citizens do, to the common purse. All wealth should be subject to the principle that, as its making benefits from the general conditions provided by states and societies within which that wealth is made, businesses and individuals who thereby profit from the state's provision (the state educates their workforce, protects their patents and contracts, enacts laws that prevent their competitors from undermining their activities, and so much more) should make their fair contribution to those states through taxation.

Finally: one great hope for democracy on the part of its first proponents was that a world of democracies would be a peaceful one. The trope that 'democracies don't go to war *with each other*' is not universally true, but as the extensive literature of 'peace and conflict studies' suggests, the degree to which it fails to be true is associated with the low position on indices of democracy occupied by mutually-combating democracies.[9] As authoritarianism increases across the world and within current democracies, the prospect of conflict itself increases. Being bombed is one ultimate form of the negation of human rights, civil liberties and the rule of law – democracy's jewels. But it does not take bombs alone to do this. It is happening before our eyes in places that until lately prided themselves on being democracies, because of the anti-democratic factors discussed in these pages. It is not too late to fight back. But fight back we must. By reforming our democracies so that they embody the constitutional imperative – thus directing government to the service of all and preventing cliques or individuals from arrogating power to themselves – government can truly be *for the people.*

APPENDIX I

Here are two examples of 'what might have been' if, in the decade preceding this writing, statesmanship were available. One is less probable or even possible than the other, perhaps; but they are examples nonetheless.

The less probable one is that on being elected to the presidency Joe Biden said, 'Our electoral system is not fit for purpose. Plurality voting for the House of Representatives entrenches a two-party binary that has become a source of bitter division. The Senate is not democratic at all, and is a near-permanent drag on progress. The Electoral College is a useless obstruction to the will of the people; the presidency, candidates for which should meet the standards required of anyone seeking appointment to high office in the public or private sectors, should be chosen on the popular vote, and big money should not be allowed to buy the White House. The Supreme Court needs to be genuinely independent, with people on the bench who make decisions on the merits of cases they consider, not on party political lines. I will not seek a second term to benefit from any changes; instead I will work at restructuring our system into a democracy fit for our times: more representative, more diverse, with more voices and interests being heard, thus fairer and more responsive, and less hostage to vested interests.'

His fight would have been with vested political and financial interests, not with the people of the US.

The other example, and one that was not only possible but should actually have happened, is that after the Brexit referendum of 2016 in the UK the then Prime Minister, David Cameron, should have said, 'This was an advisory referendum, an opinion poll, on a highly complex and consequential matter. In it thirty-seven per cent of the electorate (twenty-six per cent of the population) voted to leave the EU. Our law does not allow a trades union to hold a strike unless a minimum threshold of forty per cent of all members votes for it. Our House of Commons cannot dissolve to a general election outside the parliamentary term unless sixty-six per cent of all MPs agree, given the significant consequences that might follow if a change of government results. Accordingly Parliament must debate the outcome of the referendum, and decide whether or not the advice of just over a third of the electorate should be followed.' Such a debate was never called; instead Cameron, having painted himself into a corner by announcing before the referendum that, although the referendum was not mandating, he would nevertheless act as if it were, resigned and his party immediately behaved as if it had that mandate.

On the day of the referendum vote, after a campaign soiled by untruths, social media manipulation, outside interference

APPENDIX I

and illegal spending by the Leave campaign, with significant numbers of people having a vital interest in the outcome excluded from participation, and with significant numbers of others not voting either because they were indifferent to whether the UK stayed in the EU or not, or were convinced that no one would be unwise enough to vote to leave, 51.89 per cent of votes cast were for Leave. On the crudest application of the majoritarian fallacy, this was taken as decisive.[1] The result of what was not just a failure of nerve but an abdication of responsibility has since been painfully manifested in the UK's rapid and serious economic decline and international marginalisation. I have told this melancholy story at greater length, with the relevant evidence in full, in *Democracy and Its Crisis*.

APPENDIX II

'THE CHALLENGE OF FAR-RIGHT IDEOLOGY TO DEMOCRACY AND HUMAN RIGHTS IN EUROPE'

Report[1]
Committee on Political Affairs and Democracy
Doc. 15826
20 September 2023
Rapporteur: Mr Samad SEYIDOV, Azerbaijan, European Conservatives Group and Democratic Alliance

Summary

In view of the increase in recent years of far-right violence, driven by xenophobia, racism and other forms of intolerance, the report outlines the threats these actions pose to human rights, to the functioning of democratic institutions, and to diverse and inclusive societies.

APPENDIX II

To counter these challenges to the fundamental values that the Council of Europe aims to uphold, the report calls for strengthened adherence to these values. This includes fortifying legislation to counter far-right extremism, enhancing education and media literacy, and combating online radicalisation.

The draft resolution underlines that politicians and political parties should be at the forefront of responses to far-right extremism, both in the public defence of human rights and democratic principles, and in the unequivocal rejection of all forms of racism and intolerance, hate speech, incitement to racial hatred and harassment. It calls for a respectful and inclusive dialogue, and encourages political parties to sign the Charter of European political parties for a non-racist and inclusive society.

Contents

A. Draft resolution
B. Explanatory memorandum by Mr Samad Seyidov, rapporteur
    1. Introduction
        1.1 Background and origin
        1.2 Scope of the report
    2. Defining the far-right extremist ideology
    3. Key drivers and trends of far-right extremism
        3.1 Violent far-right extremism: a growing threat that is increasingly transnational

3.2 The online extremist environment
3.3 Far-right ideology mainstreamed
4. The challenge of far-right ideology to our common values
4.1 Undermining democratic norms
4.2 Undermining human rights
5. Tackling the threat
5.1 Legal responses
5.2 Cultural-societal responses
6. Conclusions

A. Draft resolution[2]

1. Ideologies that seek to repudiate democracy, undermine human rights and ignore the rule of law are in direct opposition to the core values of the Council of Europe. The attacks of recent years by far-right extremists, both in Europe and globally, must serve as a signal of the danger posed by this ideology to human rights, the functioning of democratic institutions, and to diverse and inclusive societies.
2. The Parliamentary Assembly recalls the commitments taken by Council of Europe member States to abide by the principles of democracy, human rights and the rule of law, and to uphold pluralism, tolerance and respect for diversity as fundamental values that underpin European societies. Extremist ideologies that threaten these principles and commitments warrant a coherent and

APPENDIX II

responsible approach in order to preserve a free, secure, and democratic Europe.

3. Far-right violence, driven by xenophobia, racism and other forms of intolerance, has increased sharply in recent years. Failed coup attempts from Germany to Brazil and attacks on elected representatives have further demonstrated the growing danger of far-right extremism, while a number of member States consider forms of far-right terrorism the fastest growing or most prominent domestic security threat they face.

4. The Assembly has repeatedly made clear its unequivocal condemnation of manifestations of far-right extremism. It has adopted a number of resolutions to tackle the challenge of extreme right-wing ideology, hate speech and intolerance. The evolving dynamics of modern far-right movements, the more sophisticated means of communication, the proliferation of online extremist material, the mainstreaming of the far-right ideology into the public domain, and the raised threat levels across a number of member States mean that it is necessary to continue to refine and adapt actions to protect against ideologies that are incompatible with human rights, democracy and the rule of law.

5. A continuing pattern of democratic backsliding in Europe provides a backdrop for the rise in actions that are against our core values and standards. The Assembly considers that the most effective way of preventing far-right extremism is to strengthen adherence to these core values.

6. The Fourth Summit of the Heads of State and Government of the Council of Europe has given renewed

impetus to the Organisation as the cornerstone of European democratic security, to the protection of our democratic foundations, and to countering challenges to human rights. The Assembly welcomes the resolve of member States to stand firm against authoritarian tendencies by enhancing shared commitments.

7. Politicians and political parties should be at the forefront of responses to the phenomenon, both in the public defence of human rights and democratic principles and in the unequivocal rejection of all forms of racism and intolerance, hate speech, incitement to racial hatred and harassment.

8. Governments must ensure that there are counterweights to extremist discourse by publicly challenging the narratives of far-right extremism, and ensuring that measures are in place that strengthen the respect of human rights and promote a model of society that embraces diversity and respects human dignity.

9. Comprehensive approaches to tackle far-right extremist ideologies are needed that seek to engage all levels of society in preventing and countering violent extremism. The Assembly emphasises the need for national action plans against extremist ideologies that include whole-of-society approaches, involving civil society, the media, educational institutions, and political parties.

10. In light of reports of the elevated risk of youth radicalisation in recent years, the Assembly recalls the importance of education as a bulwark against the spread of far-right extremist ideologies, and the continued need to

enhance societal resilience against extremist materials and recruitment in response to the extensive use of online platforms to promote extremist ideologies.

11. The Assembly recognises the vital role played in democracies by law enforcement personnel. While it is the case that the overwhelming majority of police officers reject extremism in all its forms, the exposure of far-right extremists in police forces in a number of member States in recent years is a cause for serious concern. Individuals who reject the democratic foundations of the State cannot serve it, and the Assembly emphasises the need to ensure effective mechanisms are implemented against extremists in the police.

12. The Assembly considers that, in light of the transnational nature of the phenomenon, enhanced co-operation between member States is necessary to tackle the pan-European dimension of the threat, and urges member States to engage in international co-operation and information sharing to effectively counter cross-border activities of far-right extremist groups.

13. The Assembly attaches great importance to the work of the bodies of the Council of Europe, notably through the European Commission against Racism and Intolerance, in the monitoring, standard setting, and co-operation activities for combating discrimination, racism and intolerance in our societies.

14. In the light of these considerations, the Assembly calls on Council of Europe member States to:
    14.1. review and, if necessary, enhance existing legislation to effectively counter far-right extremism as

well as hate speech, incitement to violence, and discrimination propagated by far-right individuals and groups;

14.2. strengthen existing measures to protect groups in vulnerable and marginalised situations from discrimination, harassment, and violence stemming from far-right ideologies;

14.3. promote education and media literacy by integrating comprehensive education about human rights, diversity, and democracy into school curricula, and enhance media literacy programmes to empower citizens to critically analyse and resist extremist propaganda;

14.4. combat online radicalisation through collaboration with social media platforms and tech companies to identify and remove online content that promotes far-right ideologies, while safeguarding freedom of expression and avoiding undue censorship;

14.5. develop strategies to counter disinformation and propaganda propagated by far-right groups, ensuring that accurate and evidence-based information prevails;

14.6. continue to support civil society by providing adequate financial and moral support to civil society organisations and grassroots initiatives working to promote tolerance, intercultural understanding, social cohesion, and deradicalisation;

14.7. encourage political leaders to engage in respectful and inclusive public discourse, condemning hate speech and divisive rhetoric, and advocating for policies that uphold democratic values and human rights;

14.8. enhance the protection of elected officials from politically motivated crimes, intimidation and threats.

15. To this end, the Assembly calls on member States:

15.1. as regards legislation to counter far-right extremism and to enhance the protection of groups in vulnerable and marginalised situations, to:

15.1.1. ensure legislation that addresses the dissolution of political parties or prohibition of the formation of a political party complies with the jurisprudence of the European Court of Human Rights and the recommendations of the European Commission for Democracy through Law;

15.1.2. elaborate potential strategies to prosecute violent extremism conducive to terrorism;

15.1.3. sign and ratify, if they have not already done so, Protocol No. 12 to the Convention for the Protection of Human Rights and Fundamental Freedoms (ETS No. 177) and the Additional Protocol to the Convention on Cybercrime, concerning the criminalisation of acts of a racist and xenophobic nature committed through computer systems (ETS No. 189);

15.1.4. disseminate and fully implement Recommendation CM/Rec(2022)16 of the Committee of Ministers to member States on combating hate speech;
15.1.5. set up anti-hate crime units in police forces;
15.1.6. ensure effective mechanisms for taking action against law enforcement personnel engaged in far-right extremist activities;

15.2. as regards the promotion of education and media literacy, combating online radicalisation and countering disinformation, to:

15.2.1. counteract extremist narratives and various forms of incitement, in line with Assembly Resolution 2221 (2018) 'Counter-narratives to terrorism', through school programmes and awareness-raising campaigns, underlining the shared values of human dignity, peace, non-violence, tolerance and human rights, and involve the victims of extremist acts;
15.2.2. develop a co-ordinated national media literacy policy, in line with Assembly Resolution 2314 (2019) 'Media education in the new media environment';
15.2.3. support educational projects and teaching methods aimed at tackling anti-democratic ideologies;
15.2.4. supplement public messaging and awareness campaigns by taking active measures

APPENDIX II

> to address conspiracy theories and disinformation and enhance fact-checking capabilities as part of a package of measures to enhance societal resilience against far-right propaganda;
>
> 15.2.5. ensure that internet intermediaries take effective measures to fulfil their duties and responsibilities not to make accessible or disseminate hate speech that is prohibited under criminal, civil or administrative law;
>
> 15.3. as regards supporting civil society, to:
>
> 15.3.1. support prevention policies, including through engagement with entities that work directly with the youth, such as social workers and mental health workers;
>
> 15.3.2. deepen partnerships with civil society organisations that are engaged with deradicalisation, rehabilitation, and victim support;
>
> 15.4. as regards upholding a respectful and inclusive political discourse, to:
>
> 15.4.1. implement the European Commission against Racism and Intolerance General Policy Recommendation No. 15 on Combating Hate Speech by adopting relevant administrative, civil and, as a last resort, criminal law provisions;
>
> 15.4.2. ensure that no public funding is allocated to parties promoting hate speech and hate crime;

15.5. as regards enhancing the protection of elected officials, to elaborate, in co-ordination with them, specific measures to improve their protection.
16. The Assembly, in calling for a respectful and inclusive political dialogue, encourages its members to speak out against all forms of intolerance, and political parties to sign the Charter of European political parties for a non-racist and inclusive society as endorsed in its Resolution 2443 (2022) 'The role of political parties in fostering diversity and inclusion: a new charter for a non-racist society'.
17. The Assembly invites international organisations which share the Council of Europe's values, starting with the European Union and the Organization for Security and Co-operation in Europe, to increase their co-operation with the Council of Europe in order to find common solutions to the shared problem of far-right extremism.

B. Explanatory memorandum by Mr Samad Seyidov, rapporteur

1. Introduction

1.1. Background and origin
1. In its Resolution 1344 (2003) 'Threat posed to democracy by extremist parties and movements in Europe', drawing attention to the trend of political extremism

APPENDIX II

in Europe, the Parliamentary Assembly encouraged Council of Europe member States to be more vigilant than ever and to assess the threats posed by extremism to the fundamental values that the Council of Europe aims to uphold. To counteract the harmful effects of extremism and to preserve the rule of law based on respect for democratic principles and human rights, the Assembly recommended that member States adopt a set of legislative and administrative measures, as well as measures in the field of political ethics and education. It also stressed that to be effective, such measures should benefit from the backing of public opinion and be supported by civil society.

2. Twenty years later, the Committee on Political Affairs and Democracy (the committee) set out to prepare a report on 'The challenge of far-right ideology to democracy and human rights in Europe', with a view to elaborating recommendations aimed at hindering the spread of the ideology of intolerance throughout Europe and eradicating impunity for acts of intimidation and violence committed by representatives of far-right movements.[3] The truth is that over the past two decades the far-right ideology has risen and rapidly spread both in Europe, and globally. Recent illustrations of this include the arrest, in December 2022, of dozens associated with the far-right Reichsbürger movement (citizens of the Reich) on suspicion of plotting a coup against the German Government. In January 2023, in a grim echo of the US Capitol invasion by backers of

former President Donald Trump in 2021, hundreds of right-wing extremist protesters, supporters of former President Jair Bolsonaro, invaded and vandalised places of power in Brasília (Brazil).
3. The pillars of our democratic security – an efficient and independent judiciary; freedom of expression; freedom of assembly and association; the efficient functioning of democratic institutions; and the construction of an inclusive society and democratic citizenship – are all threatened by extremist ideology. Both the Assembly in its resolutions[4] and the member States of the Council of Europe have called this democratic security key for securing peace and prosperity in Europe, and have resultantly committed to countering actions that undermine human rights, democracy, and the rule of law. This was notably reiterated in the Reykjavík Declaration of the Council of Europe Fourth Summit of the Heads of State and Government (Reykjavík Declaration).[5] Against this background, this report is timelier than ever.

1.2. Scope of the report

4. Following my appointment as rapporteur in September 2021, the committee held a first exchange of views on this issue on 16 March 2022. During this exchange, members noted that the far-right ideology was a serious threat not only to democracy, but also to international peace and stability. Stressing that violence or hatred in political discourse and activity should be fully rejected,

members cautioned against the manipulation for political purposes of labels such as 'extremist' or 'far-right' for political parties, which should not be used lightly.

5. In a further exchange of views held by the committee on 27 April 2023, opinions were divided. While some members thought that I should focus the report on the far-right ideology, others drew my attention to far-left extremism and suggested that I expand the scope of the report to cover all forms of extreme ideologies.

6. I agree that left-wing extremism trends should continue to be followed: it is a phenomenon that continues to affect the continent, with Europol reports for the period 2006–2020 showing over 414 failed, foiled or completed attacks in European Union countries inspired by extreme left-wing and anarchist ideology.[6] A large part of these attacks resulted in vandalism and destruction of property, and several important instances have seen injuries and human casualties.[7] These ideologies have been recognised in the Council of Europe Counter-Terrorism Strategy (2023–2027) as an issue of concern for some countries, though the threat of violent far-left extremism across Europe has been considered low.[8]

7. Having attentively considered both views, I have decided to follow the scope laid down in the original motion. I have reached this conclusion not only because far-right ideology has a particular historical legacy in Europe but also because it is considered the fastest growing threat in many European countries, as highlighted by the Council of Europe's Committee on

Counter Terrorism.[9] In the spirit of the motion for a resolution at its origin, this report will focus on the manifestations of far-right ideology that are in clear contradiction to the principles and values of the Council of Europe, which the motion notes as an expansion of intolerance, hate speech and discrimination which is often accompanied by acts of intimidation and violence. It is this extremist threat that the report will address.

8. During the preparation of the report, on 25 January 2023, the committee held a hearing with the participation of two experts: Dr Cynthia Miller-Idriss, Founding Director, Polarization and Extremism Research and Innovation Lab, American University, Professor, School of Public Affairs and School of Education, Washington (USA), and Mr Nicholas Potter, journalist and researcher of the far-right at the Amadeu Antonio Foundation (Berlin). A second hearing was held on 20 June 2023 with the participation of Mr Nicos Alivizatos (Greece), member of the European Commission for Democracy through Law (Venice Commission).

2. Defining the far-right extremist ideology

9. There is not a universally agreed definition of far-right extremism. As an umbrella term, it can encompass a heterogeneous set of ideologies, beliefs and narratives. For the purposes of this report, three defining characteristics are outlined, that are to all be present to fulfil

APPENDIX II

classification as far-right extremism. First, a belief in some form of natural inequality or hierarchy between peoples or groups of people, which may include nationalism, nativism, racism, xenophobia, antisemitism, Islamophobia, and homophobia. Second, a belief in authoritarianism. Third, an implicit or explicit aim to destroy the democratic system.[10]

10. Within the far-right, scholars usually distinguish between the 'radical' and the 'extreme' right. Radical right groups and organisations, while operating within the democratic processes, accepting popular sovereignty and the minimal procedural rules of parliamentary democracy, are hostile to liberal democracy and criticise its crucial aspects, such as pluralism and minority rights, and publicly condemn the use of violence as an instrument of politics.

11. By contrast, a key feature of extreme far-right groups and organisations is the rejection of the underlying values of democracies and the rule of law.[11] The behavioural characteristic that therefore distinguishes the radical and the extreme right is the legitimisation of the use of violence by the latter to pursue their aims. This threat or use of harassment or violence have been stated to be important features of far-right extremism.[12] They include terrorist attacks, hate crime, spontaneous violence, hate speech, and incitement to violence or hatred.[13] Contemporary examples of extreme right actors include Golden Dawn in Greece, and the white supremacist groups in the United States.[14]

12. The report therefore uses this prism of ideology accompanied by the behavioural characteristic of the legitimisation of the use of violence to define the phenomenon.

13. In addition to being ideologically complex, the far-right is organisationally varied. Aside from political parties, there are a range of sub-party groupings with far-right sympathies, including relatively formal organisations such as think thanks, pressure groups, media organisations, as well as more ad hoc groups, including forums, street organisations, online and offline communities. Increasingly, the far-right space is defined by networks rather than formal organisations, with individuals maintaining multiple ties and avoiding formal membership. The far-right is also composed in large part of lone activists developing, following and promoting their own position from individual platforms.[15] The Council of Europe Committee on Counter-Terrorism has described this as a growing trend of 'post-organisational activity', where individuals and groups operate independently of each other and never report to a central headquarter or single leader for direction or instruction.[16]

14. The lack of an agreed definition of far-right ideology places some barriers to effectively countering and responding to the phenomenon, and for understanding and measuring the scale of the issue across different member States. The partial overlap between hate crime, violent far-right extremism and far-right terrorism

complicates how certain actions are prosecuted, and resultantly how governments may assess the number of violent far-right attacks committed on their territory.

3. Key drivers and trends of far-right extremism

15. Right-wing extremism is a recurring phenomenon that has grown in recent decades. Its appearance and operation do not exist in a vacuum, but are a response to interlinking socio-economic and cultural factors, building on real or perceived changes in society.[17] In the last twenty years, the world has faced a succession of crises – in global finance, migration, the Covid-19 pandemic and the return of a large-scale war of aggression on the European continent – with grave social, economic and political consequences, leading to frustration, fear and anger. Experts have argued that this is key to understanding the rising support for far-right extremism, including its violent manifestations.
16. Indeed, relying on social discontent, extremism proposes simplistic and stereotyped solutions in response to the anxieties and uncertainties affecting our societies. It shifts responsibility for these difficulties to the inability of democracy to meet the challenges of today's world, and the incapacity of elected representatives and institutions to address citizens' expectations. Alternatively, discrimination is incited against specific groups by blaming them for insecurity and

socio-economic problems, or suggesting they are a potential threat to the state.[18]

17. The economic insecurity perspective has also been paired with further currents of support to far-right extremism emanating as a reaction against perceived or real cultural changes that threaten the worldview of previously predominant sectors of the population.[19] Interactive processes between the socio-economic and cultural factors combine to lead parts of society challenge [sic] the legitimacy of democracies.

18. Intelligence services have noted the evolving features of the far-right milieu in recent years, with traditional forms of the far-right such as neo-Nazism and skinhead culture being overtaken in certain States by anti-Islam and anti-migrant activism as the most prevalent topics of far-right extremism.[20] The evolving trends have also seen a more radically anti-establishment shift, with far-right extremists increasingly targeting institutions, with an acceleration of this trend following the onset of the Covid-19 pandemic.

19. Further risks factors [sic] associated to the emergence of manifestations of right-wing extremism have been identified as unresolved identity-related issues, systemic poor governance, and administrative dysfunction. This can be compounded by low trust in mainstream media, low media literacy, and a lack of critical and independent journalism which, combined, can amplify vulnerability to disinformation.[21]

APPENDIX II

20. In 2021, the European Commission against Racism and Intolerance (ECRI), voiced its alarm of the use of inflammatory rhetoric and the dissemination of hateful and dehumanising content, and recalled that the failure to prevent and combat ultra-nationalistic and racist hate speech can lead to grave violations of the European Convention on Human Rights (ETS No. 5) and a descent into violence.[22]

21. It is a matter of deep common concern when ideologies advocate for the use of violence or other unlawful activity to promote particular beliefs. The use of ideological language that may vilify or discriminate against others is one manifestation of this.

3.1. Violent far-right extremism: a growing threat that is increasingly transnational

22. The far-right landscape stretches to all corners of the world. While its salience in Europe has grown considerably throughout the 2000s, it has both a historical and contemporary presence in Latin America, India and Indonesia, as well as in North America and Oceania.[23]

23. The violent manifestations of far-right ideology are also global. Today, political violence associated with the far-right is widely seen as a growing threat across the globe.[24] The Report on Emerging Terrorist Threats in Europe, prepared under the auspices of the Council of Europe Committee on Counter-Terrorism (CDCT),

confirms it for Europe, stressing that far-right terrorism is a growing threat across a number of member States.[25]

24. In recent years, in addition to mass shootings (Utøya, Norway, 2011; Charlottesville, USA, 2017; Christchurch, New Zealand, 2019), far-right extremists carried out acts of political assassination (British member of Parliament Jo Cox, 2016; German politician Walter Lübcke, 2019) and insurrection, including armed insurrection (US Capitol Invasion, 2021; and most recently the insurrection in Brazil) or plotted to do so (Germany, 2022). The continued extremist threat has also been manifested in the attacks on mosques, synagogues, and asylum reception centres witnessed in Europe in the past years.

25. The growing transnational character of violent far-right extremism is also due to increased co-operation between extremist groups and networks sharing motives, inspirations, and goals online and offline, across different countries.[26] Conclusions of the International Conference on 'Transnational Terrorist Threats from Emerging and Re-emerging Violent Extremist Movements' confirm that online platforms are extensively used for recruitment and spreading extremist ideologies as well as instructional material. This allows groups and individuals to learn and take inspiration from each other.[27] Loosely organised, online networks are increasingly a means by which violent far-right actors engage with other individuals and groups internationally, with lone actors inspired by these

networks or groups being the main tactic for carrying out violent attacks. Motivated by violent extremist propaganda, these self-activating actors pose significant challenges for timely detection and interception.[28]

26. In 2011, the terrorist attack perpetrated by a far-right extremist in Oslo and on the island of Utøya, in Norway, which left 77 people dead, shocked the world. A few years later, another far-right extremist, drawing on the extreme ideas and action of the perpetrator of [the] Utøya attacks, would kill 51 people Muslim worshippers [sic] at the other end of the world, in Christchurch, New Zealand. Months later, another far-right extremist 'inspired' by the Christchurch gunman killed two people in Halle, Germany. These 'copycat' manifestations of far-right extremism show the danger of what social psychologists have referred to as behavioural contagion, and the global reach of far-right extremist violence.[29]

27. There are also continuing concerns about the infiltration of far-right ideology in the military, armed forces and law enforcement, and the circulation of far-right extremist materials in these groups. In this context, it is worth noting that amongst those arrested in the framework of the plot against the German Government, there was a judge and former members of the military, including from the special forces. Cases against law enforcement and security agents for both the preparation of terrorist attacks directed against politicians and public figures, and for affiliation with proscribed groups have

taken place in recent years. Similarly, it is argued that the insurrection in Brazil was possible because of collusion with parts of the military police hierarchy. It goes without saying that there is a particular threat when those who are in charge of safeguarding and protecting citizens are influenced by extremist ideologies.

3.2. *The online extremist environment*

28. Since the Assembly last visited this subject in Resolution 1344 (2003), technological advances have further facilitated the international networking efforts of far-right extremists. Social media and online gaming platforms, as well as wider internet subcultures, are largely used to spread an extreme right-wing ideology and to target individuals for recruitment.[30] The sharp increase in online material promoting far-right ideologies has amplified radicalisation processes and removed the need for 'real-life' contact.

29. The online environment has seen the proliferation of content including performative propaganda, 'manifestos', memes, videos popularising far-right extremism by influencers, and online ideological literature. Challenges exist in both the moderation of online spaces, with extremists able to migrate to a range of platforms with differing regulatory structures, and the use of coded messaging between groups, which has been described as pushing the boundaries of freedom of expression to its fullest extent, making it difficult for law enforcement agencies to intervene using existing tools.[31]

30. The way people spend time online can have important effects. The risk of online radicalisation is increased by echo chambers where extreme content is self-reinforcing across platforms. Algorithmic radicalisation, where algorithms on social media sites drive users towards progressively more extreme content, can lead to so-called 'rabbit holes' of disinformation, conspiracy theories and propaganda consumption.

31. The Covid-19 pandemic has contributed to the amplification of far-right narratives online, with manifestations of this being the marked global rise in anti-Asian and antisemitic conspiracy theories. The pandemic also contributed to the emergence of new ideologies and cross-pollination between disparate ideological groups and demographics. Multiple grievances related to pandemic responses, generalised sentiments of fear, anxiety, and uncertainty, as well as increased isolation have provided an environment for exploitation by far-right movements looking to transfer fears and frustrations onto targeted 'other' individuals and groups. This was accompanied in an uplift in the amount of time online that provided conditions for the circulation of propaganda and disinformation, and the consequent elevated risk of online radicalisation.

3.3. Far-right ideology mainstreamed

32. It is crucial to position extremism as a threat to democracy itself. It is both a direct threat because it jeopardises the democratic constitutional order and freedoms, and

an indirect threat because it can distort political life. In 2003, the Assembly warned against traditional political parties being potentially tempted to adopt the stance and the demagogic discourse specific to extremist parties in order to counter the increasing electoral popularity of the latter. Also in 2010, the Assembly expressed concern about the non-negligible risk that mainstream political parties tend to rely on racist discourse in order to avoid losing part of their electorate.[32] These are signals that our democracies are not immune to far-right politics. Most recently, the Assembly noted that hate speech and intolerance had become part of political discourse, where they are used not only by populist and extremist groups but increasingly by representatives of movements and parties across the political spectrum.[33] This is a worrying trend that must be stopped.

33. The Assembly has noted the important role of political parties in contributing to the fight against racism and intolerance, and to foster an inclusive society. The Revised Charter of European political parties for a non-racist and inclusive society commits signatories to defend basic human rights and democratic principles and reject all forms of racism and intolerance, hate speech, incitement to racial hatred and harassment.[34] I encourage all political parties to sign the Revised Charter, as a sign of their commitment to Council of Europe values.

APPENDIX II

34. Sensitive balances exist for the media. Newsrooms are confronted by the question of how to fulfil their democratic role of informing the public while avoiding giving disproportionate weight to extremists or key far-right personalities. Inadvertently providing an outsized platform to marginal extremist views risks legitimising and advancing these ideas and their aims.

4. The challenge of far-right ideology to our common values

4.1. Undermining democratic norms

35. The spread of extreme ideas, both offline and online and their increased acceptance pose a grave threat to the democratic legal order.
36. Events such as the storming of the US Capitol in 2021 demonstrate the continuing and active threat far-right ideologies has [sic] globally. The activities of a militant fringe were instrumental in provoking the mobilisation of thousands of people who attempted to overturn the result of a legitimate election.
37. Attacks on the constitutional order, such as those directed against the judiciary or electoral processes, as well as actions that aim to degrade or subvert our democratic culture are a rising concern. Both implicit and explicit attempts to weaken the checks and balances of

public institutions are a threat to democracy, and the Council of Europe has repeatedly warned of this threat of democratic backsliding. In the commitment to the Reykjavik Principles at the Fourth Summit of the Heads of State and Government of the Council of Europe in May 2023, member States agreed to protect and promote the principles of democracy, rule of law and human rights, to stand firm against authoritarian tendencies, and prevent and resist democratic backsliding in Europe.

38. Violent manifestations of extremism are fundamentally repudiations in themselves of our shared democratic values of tolerance, respect, inclusion and diversity. The functioning of the democratic order is impaired via manifestations of extremism such as systematic hate speech, fearmongering, spreading disinformation, demonisation, and intimidation.[35]

39. Efforts to exert influence became particularly pronounced in demonstrations against Covid-19 measures, with public demonstrations seeing the appearance of non-affiliated groups of far-right ideologues attacking the legitimacy of government action, democratic institutions, and amplifying conspiracy theories. The use of violence at a number of these events and the abuse of the right to protest are not acceptable.

40. Incidents of harassment of elected officials and threats posed to them have been co-ordinated by far-right groups. This intimidation cannot be tolerated in our democratic culture.

APPENDIX II

4.2. Undermining human rights

41. Human rights are based on the premise of the inherent dignity and equality of all human beings and so promoting one set of rights while undermining or violating the rights of others is antithetical to human rights principles.

42. Far-right ideologies encompass and promote xenophobic, racist, nativist visions, including other forms of intolerance or in the name of religion or belief. The 'othering' of people considered to be in an out-group sees such groups the target of hatred, and denies their human rights. So-called 'grievance narratives' put certain individuals and communities at particular risk. This includes ethnic and religious groups, the LGBTQ community, as well as politicians and other public figures.[36] Hate speech, calls for restrictive policies that infringe the human rights of minority groups, and the spread of an ideology of intolerance must be addressed.

5. Tackling the threat

43. The presence and threat of non-democratic groups mean that steps need to be taken to reinforce democracies. The internationalisation of far-right ideology, the outsized role of online extremist content, and the mainstreaming of far-right extremism put an accent on the need to address disinformation, misinformation, and

propaganda. The risk of key democratic tenets being undermined is too great to not act.

44. This should be done, *inter alia*, by strengthening democratic values and practices within the mainstream, and taking action via both [*sic*] legal, political and educational strategies. The concept of 'defensive democracy' (also referred to as 'militant democracy') can be instructive for these actions, being defined as 'all activities, be these formal provisions or political strategies, which are explicitly and directly aimed at protecting the democratic system from the threat of its internal opponents'.[37]

45. These 'defensive democracy' measures take a number of forms. First, through legislation that curbs threats to the democratic order and its key principles of human rights, democracy and the rule of law. Second, through cultural-societal responses, that is to say educational and social strategies that build resilience against susceptibility to propaganda, disinformation and persuasive extremist techniques including scapegoating. This includes strategies to give people the tools to build their own counter-arguments, recognise and reject misinformation, as well as supporting the important role played by civil society in these efforts.[38]

5.1. Legal responses

46. In efforts to combat the threat of extremism effectively, member States have developed a number of legislative measures to address both far-right extremism and

activities linked to it. As well as codifying criminal activity with extremist aspects, member States have also developed legislation to address threats to the democratic or constitutional order.

5.1.1. Hate speech

47. Where organisations have been found to engage in acts such as hate speech, discrimination, and violence, member States have taken steps to disband these organisations, such as action taken by the French government in 2021 against the organisation Génération Identitaire; the decree of the Supreme Court of Finland of 22 September 2020 that the Nordic Resistance Movement and Pohjoinen Perinne ry (Northern Tradition) were to be disbanded; the proscription of National Action in the United Kingdom in 2016; and the recognition of the organisation Golden Dawn as a criminal organisation in Greece in October 2020.

48. The legislation related to the disbanding of far-right extremist organisations can take a number of forms, such as laws on association and hate-crime offences, and with regards to proscription where organisations are believed to be concerned in terrorism. With similar challenges being faced across Europe, and in light of the transnational aspects of the threat, there is a continued need for co-operation and work towards common legal

approaches. Increasing support to national authorities to co-ordinate cross-border investigations, and knowledge sharing by relevant investigatory bodies on best practice of how to conduct investigations and prosecutions of far-right extremism would be helpful measures to enhance this co-operation.

49. In relation to online extremist content, greater government intervention has been noted in recent years with a growing number of governments proposing and enacting laws to counter the proliferation of terrorist and extremist content online.[39] Online content-sharing services tend to prohibit themselves the use of their technologies to engage in violent extremist activities, and further co-operation with these services could help support the co-ordination of approaches to the definitions of violent extreme contents to bring further clarity to these efforts.

50. In response to a persistent and worrying increase in hate speech, especially online, and documented by the monitoring bodies of the Council of Europe, the Committee of Ministers has adopted recommendations on combating the phenomenon, including calls to establish comprehensive and effective legal frameworks that consist of appropriately calibrated provisions of civil, administrative and criminal law. The Committee of Ministers recommends that criminal law provisions in relation to hate speech should only be applied as a last resort and for the most serious expressions of hatred.[40]

APPENDIX II

5.1.2. Restrictions on political parties

51. Developed in reaction to concerns that anti-democratic and extremist elements may attempt to enter the democratic institutions of a country in order to abuse and subvert the democratic order, a range of mechanisms monitor, contain and prosecute extremist rhetoric and activity. Relevant instruments include measures that constrain directly or indirectly the presence of extremist and anti-democratic groups within democratic institutions.

52. Recommendations from the ECRI have included the withdrawal of all financial and other forms of support by public bodies from political parties and other organisations that use hate speech or fail to sanction its use by members. Member States should also provide, while respecting the right to freedom of association, for the possibility of prohibiting or dissolving such organisations where the use of hate speech is intended or can be expected to incite acts of violence, intimidation, hostility or discrimination against those targeted by it.[41]

53. The Assembly has stated that 'restrictions on or dissolution of political parties should be regarded as exceptional measures to be applied only in cases where the party concerned uses violence or threatens civil peace and the democratic constitutional order of the country', and that 'as far as possible, less radical measures than dissolution should be used'.[42] This has been echoed by the Venice Commission who recommended that 'the

competence of state authorities to dissolve a political party or prohibit one from being formed should concern exceptional circumstances, must be narrowly tailored and should be applied only in extreme cases. Such a high level of protection is appropriate, given the fundamental role of political parties in the democratic process that also requires a stricter level of scrutiny in comparison with other associations than political parties'.[43]

54. Measures restricting or dissolving political parties have been imposed by a number of European countries. In February 2023, the Greek Parliament took legislative steps to disqualify parties led by politicians convicted of serious offences and are [sic] deemed a potential threat to democracy from standing for election. These measures were upheld by a ruling of 2 May 2023 by the Supreme Court of Greece. In this, the Supreme Court decided to disqualify the Hellenes National Party due to the incitation of violence, disrespect to democracy, the promotion of totalitarian ideologies, the dissemination of racist and intolerant ideas and hatred that threatened the peaceful coexistence of social groups in the country.[44]

55. Further examples of adjudication by constitutional courts on the issue of the prohibition of a party include the 2017 decision of the German Federal Constitutional Court that ruled against banning the National Democratic Party of Germany.[45] The National Democratic Party advocates for the abolition of the existing free democratic basic order and for replacing it

with an authoritarian national State that adheres to the idea of an ethnically defined community. The reasoning of the Constitutional Court included assessing whether there were specific and weighty indicators that a party could achieve its anti-democratic goals, and with a lack of evidence that the party in question could do so, the prohibition was not necessary for the protection of democracy.[46]

56. Democratic defence actions in themselves may raise questions about their compliance with human rights standards. While human rights instruments acknowledge the existence of valid reasons for restrictions on freedom of association, such as the need to counter violent extremism, the measures have to be the least intrusive means to achieve the respective objective. Any action taken to achieve a legitimate aim must be necessary in a democratic society, and not applied for any other purpose than those for which it has been prescribed.[47]

57. The European Court of Human Rights has consistently ruled that, due to their important role in the functioning of democracy, limitations on the formation of political parties should be used with restraint and only when necessary in a democracy.[48]

5.2. *Cultural-societal responses*

58. Combating far-right extremism requires a multi-faceted approach that combines both law-enforcement and adequate security measures, with non-legal responses

that put an accent on prevention, education, and addressing root causes.

59. In view of the transnational nature of far-right extremism, it is important to increase international co-operation as a key tool to exchange on challenges and good practices, as well as to create synergies between States, international organisations, and specialised entities. Co-ordinated multi-stakeholder efforts to map and analyse political, societal, and other drivers behind the growth of adherents to far-right ideologies are welcome measures to proactively assess and react to developments. Common definitions and practices can help enhance data collection on the scale of the threat, as well as bringing greater conceptual clarity to how to approach the phenomenon.

60. Both research and practical experience have shown the importance of engaging all levels of society in preventing and countering violent extremism.[49] The whole-of-society approach, including the involvement of public, private and non-governmental actors in tackling different aspects of radicalisation, disengagement, and social reintegration is an encouraging strategy for countering extremist narratives that pose a threat to democracy and human rights.

61. Increased investment in educational and preventative approaches to address vulnerabilities to extremist propaganda in the mainstream can be a further important measure taken by governments. The German example of the 'Demokratie leben!' (Live Democracy!)

government-funded intervention places extremism in a broader framework to strengthen and protect an inclusive, diverse democracy, and work against radicalisation and polarisation in society.[50] Proactive democratic education is an important building block for enhancing democratic resilience against the phenomena of far-right ideologies and hate speech in our societies.

62. Steps to increase societal capacity to reject all forms of extremism through formal and informal education, youth activities and the training of key players (such as the media, politicians and social actors) have been repeatedly outlined by the Council of Europe as having a crucial role in this respect.[51] Developing skills in critical thinking and media literacy can enhance resilience against disinformation, online materials that incite extremism, and recruitment efforts of far-right extremist groups.

63. Youth-targeted activities are of particular importance due to the elevated risk of youth radicalisation that has been noted in recent years. Intelligence services in some member States have observed a shift in demographic of those associated with far-right extremist activities to individuals with no criminal background, who are technically sophisticated, and increasingly under the age of 18.[52] The Reykjavík Declaration has noted the priority to be given to the participation of young persons in democratic life, including in education about human rights and core democratic values such as pluralism, inclusion and non-discrimination.[53]

64. Community groups and civil society organisations play an important role in outreach work, education, and responding to deradicalisation efforts. Co-operation and relationships between government and these groups are of continued importance for ensuring a whole-of-society approach in addressing conditions that are conducive to far-right extremism, and in efforts to prevent intolerance and violent extremism from establishing itself in communities. This includes the role of civil society organisations educating in democratic values, conducting community activity intended to strengthen democratic foundations, and helping the victims of extremist activities. It also includes the provision of support to individuals wishing to leave a violent extremist group, or to reintegrate in communities following their association with extremist groups.

65. Concern over the misuse of online space in relation to far-right extremism is both of great importance and significant complexity. A continued focus on far-right messaging, hate speech, propaganda and recruitment remains critical. At the same time, the use of coded messaging, memes, a plethora of different platforms, and encrypted communication make tracking and detection difficult. In addition, much far-right extremist content is situated among content that does not reach criminal thresholds. Further co-operation between governments and communication service providers in efforts to proactively detect and remove harmful content should be encouraged.

APPENDIX II

66. In its Resolution 2443 (2022) 'The role of political parties in fostering diversity and inclusion: a new charter for a non-racist society', the Assembly has reiterated that government representatives and politicians in general should lead efforts to eliminate racism, hatred and intolerance with resolve and set an example by publicly challenging, rejecting and condemning expressions of hatred, from whatever quarters they come. This has a vital role in promoting a model of society that embraces diversity and respects human dignity, and has a role in influencing the tone of public discourse.

67. Equally, the Assembly, in the same resolution, has called on all democratic political parties to sign and enforce the revised Charter of European political parties for a non-racist and inclusive society, which includes adherence to defending basic human rights and democratic principles and rejecting all forms of racism and intolerance, hate speech, incitement to racial hatred and harassment.

6. Conclusions

68. The Fourth Summit of the Heads of State and Government of the Council of Europe has given renewed impetus to the Organisation as the cornerstone of European democratic security, to the protection of our democratic foundations, and to countering challenges to human rights.

69. The rise and rapid spread of far-right ideology in Europe has been marked by a rise of intolerance, hate speech and discrimination – a trend that has been identified in a number of European countries as their greatest threat to democracy. We cannot accept acts of intimidation and violence that pose a risk to our democratic systems, and put human rights and fundamental freedoms in jeopardy.

70. The attacks of recent years by far-right extremists, both in Europe and globally, must equally serve as a signal that we cannot underestimate the danger posed by far-right extremism. Activities that seek to undermine democratic society, our values and our principles require a firm and robust response both at the national and international levels in order to preserve a free, secure, and democratic Europe. The challenges faced by our societies, such as economic uncertainty, societal polarisation and geopolitical instability have widened further the opportunity for far-right extremists to advertise supremacist solutions and reach disaffected audiences.

71. International co-operation and the effective implementation of coherent and responsible policies are needed to address the increasingly transnational trends, the proliferation of online extremist material, and the mainstreaming of far-right ideology into the public domain. Preventative policies need to be adapted, refined, and expanded to modern manifestations and tactics of far-right extremism.

APPENDIX II

72. Governments must ensure that there are counterweights to extremist discourse by publicly challenging them, and ensuring that education is in place that strengthens the respect of human rights and promotes understanding and tolerance.
73. Politicians should be at the forefront of this response, taking their responsibility to defend human rights and democratic principles and unequivocally reject all forms of racism and intolerance, hate speech, incitement to racial hatred and harassment.

NOTES

All website links were correct as of 31 March 2025.

Preface

1 See A.C. Grayling, *Democracy and Its Crisis* (Oneworld, 2017) and *The Good State* (Oneworld, 2020).
2 Debate and empirical data on the dilution of democracy and its constituent features of civil liberties and rights: see e.g. the assessments provided by Freedom House such as 'Democracy in Crisis': https://freedomhouse.org/report/freedom-world/2018/democracy-crisis; Saliba Sarsar and Rekha Datta (eds), *Democracy in Crisis Around the World* (Lexington Books, 2020); Mathew Nicholson, 'Democracy in Crisis: Studies Show Increasing Global Trend Towards Autocracy', *Europe Elects*, 28 March 2024: https://europeelects.eu/2024/03/28/democracy-in-crisis-studies-show-continuing-global-trend-towards-autocracy/.

NOTES

Introduction

1 This first reason is the most immediately obvious one, and widely discussed. See, for example, Richard Wike, 'Why the World is Down on Democracy', *Journal of Democracy*, Vol. 36, No. 1, 2025.
2 I describe the long and difficult process of achieving these benefits in A.C. Grayling, *Towards the Light* (Bloomsbury, 2007).

1 'Of, by, for' the People

1 James Madison, *Federalist Paper No. 10* (1787): www.sog.unc.edu/sites/www.sog.unc.edu/files/course_materials/James%20Madison%20Federlist%20Paper%2010%20Excerpts.pdf.
2 Walter Bagehot, *The English Constitution* (1867): www.gutenberg.org/cache/epub/4351/pg4351.txt.
3 Alexander Hamilton, *Federalist Paper No. 68* (1788): https://avalon.law.yale.edu/18th_century/fed68.asp.
4 Madison, *Federalist Paper No. 10*.
5 Dennis C. Rasmussen, *Fears of a Setting Sun: The Disillusionment of America's Founders* (Princeton University Press, 2021).
6 See 'How Many US Mass Shootings Have There Been in 2024?', BBC News, 17 December 2024: www.bbc.com/news/world-us-canada-41488081; Kaitlin Washburn, 'Nearly 43,000 People Died from Gun Violence in 2023: How to Tell the Story', *Association of Health Journalists*, 14 February 2024: https://healthjournalism.org/blog/2024/02/nearly-43000-people-died-from-gun-violence-in-2023-how-to-tell-the-story/.

Other countries with comparably high numbers of deaths by gun violence are Brazil and Mexico, which invites reflection on the nature of these societies, and the crime and law enforcement structures of all three, as well as the proliferation of arms in the population. See 'Gun Deaths by Country 2024', World Population Review: https://worldpopulationreview.com/country-rankings/gun-deaths-by-country.

7 'Literacy Gap Map', Barbara Bush Foundation for Family Literacy: https://map.barbarabush.org.

8 'The Share of Americans Without Health Insurance in 2023 Remained Low', Peter G. Peterson Foundation, 21 November 2024: www.pgpf.org/blog/2023/11/the-share-of-americans-without-health-insurance-in-2022-matched-a-record-low.

9 Rob LaFranco, Grace Chung and Chase Peterson-Withorn (eds), 'Forbes World's Billionaires List 2024: The Top 200', *Forbes*, 2 April 2024: www.forbes.com/sites/chasewithorn/2024/04/02/forbes-worlds-billionaires-list-2024-the-top-200/.

10 Amartya Sen in his *Idea of Justice* (Allen Lane, 2009) expressed scepticism about the degree to which institutions can counter injustices in society, as Madison and later John Rawls argued. This is because in rejecting the *homo economicus* view of people as wholly rational agents pursuing self-interest, one accepts the variability of needs and interests in society, and these are such that they cannot be met, in Sen's view, by the structure of institutions alone. This is plausible when it comes to the operation of occurrent socio-economic *policy* but misses the point being made here: that the structure of *government* has to be such as to optimise the devising and implementation of policy to ensure the optimisation

NOTES

of its outcomes. One major example is the *equality of consideration* desideratum identified by Ronald Dworkin. The constraint that institutions impose on policy derives from the explicit purposes that the institution exists to serve, these being defined constitutionally.

11 See the account of this given in my *Democracy and Its Crisis*.

12 Hailsham's speech is not readily available on the internet but is transcribed as an appendix to T.S. Ranvik's thesis 'The Many Lives of Hailsham's Famous Phrase, the Elective Dictatorship'. Hailsham modified his views after the Dimbleby occasion, settling eventually on proposals for adjusting the legal process to provide. Tonjie Sofie Ranvik, 'The Many Lives of Hailsham's Famous Phrase, the Elective Dictatorship (Master's Thesis)', University of Oslo, 2020: www.duo.uio.no/bitstream/handle/10852/80524/1/The-many-lives-of-Hailsham-s-famous-phrase--the-elective-dictatorship_-the-entire-thesis.pdf.

13 This is technically complicated in the UK in respect of the armed forces, every member of which on enlistment swears an oath of allegiance to the Crown, both its wearer and his or her heirs and successors, raising the question of which entity the military is to obey if it receives contrary commands from them: Parliament or the Crown? This is further complicated by the fact that technically 'Parliament' denotes 'the Crown, the Lords Spiritual and Temporal and the Commons' joined together in consultation – this being the arrangement settled by the 'Glorious Revolution' of 1688. This is illustrative of the messy nature of the uncodified UK constitution, which contains anomalies, unclarities and contradictions. It might seem that

since Parliament has the power to abolish the monarchy, the military has ultimately to be loyal to Parliament despite the oath to the Crown. But should the question ever be put to the test, which is exceedingly unlikely, the outcome could not be predicted with certainty; for reasons to do with military discipline and cohesion, the imperatives of loyalty (together, as it happens, with the anachronism of religious observances and allusions on occasions) make the Crown a significant focus of military identity.

14 Those who support the House of Lords as a virtually powerless delaying and revising 'second thoughts' chamber, many of whose members have valuable experience and expertise to bring to bear, criticise not the fact that its members are unelected but the fact that the method of appointment to it is too often unsatisfactory; retired members of the House of Commons are rewarded with seats in it, and under dysfunctional governments (such as that of the UK Conservative Party in the years between 2015 and 2024) corrupt appointments of wholly unsuitable individuals are made at the whim of the Prime Minister of the day, thus bringing the chamber into disrepute. But if, the House's defenders say, the appointment process were independent and focused exclusively on the merits of what a prospective member could bring in the way of expertise and experience, the chamber would continue to prove to be what it has often proved to be in recent decades, namely, an assembly where the interests of the country are held in higher regard than the interests of a political party.

NOTES

2 High Finance and Democracy

1. The World Inequality Report 2022 provides the data. 'World Inequality Report 2022', World Inequality Database: https://wir2022.wid.world.
2. In 2021, Alibaba's ecommerce gross merchandise value was $1.25 trillion; Amazon's (in second place) was $602 billion.
3. Oxfam International, 'Takers Not Makers': www.oxfam.org/en/research/takers-not-makers-unjust-poverty-and-unearned-wealth-colonialism.
4. Robert Muggah and Ian Goldin, 'COVID-19 is Increasing Multiple Kinds of Inequality. Here's What We Can Do about It', World Economic Forum, 9 October 2020: www.weforum.org/stories/2020/10/covid-19-is-increasing-multiple-kinds-of-inequality-here-s-what-we-can-do-about-it/.
5. See 'Privatising the UK's Nationalised Industries in the 1980s', Centre for Public Impact, 11 April 2016: https://centreforpublicimpact.org/public-impact-fundamentals/privatising-the-uks-nationalised-industries-in-the1980s/; 'Currents of Change: Navigating UK's Privatized Water Utilities', Bocconi Students Investment Club, 14 April 2024: https://bsic.it/currents-of-change-navigating-uks-privatized-water-utilities/; 'Rail Privatisation: Top 30 Failures in 30 Years', *We Own It*, 19 January 2023: https://weownit.org.uk/blog/rail-privatisation-top-30-failures-30-years.
6. Paul Krugman, 'The Reagan Economics Legend', *New York Times*, 11 June 2004.
7. The Investopedia Team, 'How Much US Debt Does China Own?', Investopedia, 27 July 2024: www.investopedia.com/articles/

investing/080615/china-owns-us-debt-how-much.asp. The largest holder of US debt is the US Treasury; China and Japan are the next two.

8 Richard Behar, *Madoff: The Final Word* (Avid Reader Press, 2024).
9 'Musk's $1-Million-a-Day Voter Sweepstakes Can Proceed, Says Pennsylvania Judge', *Le Monde* (with *AP*), 4 November 2024: www.lemonde.fr/en/united-states/article/2024/11/04/elon-musk-s-1-million-a-day-voter-sweepstakes-can-proceed-says-pennsylvania-judge_6731567_133.html.
10 There is a near-convergence of view from different perspectives on a 'post-capitalist' analysis: see John Kay, *The Corporation in the Twenty-First Century* (Profile Books, 2024) and Yanis Varoufakis, *Technofeudalism* (Vintage, 2023).
11 Stefania Vitali, James B. Glattfelder and Stefano Batiston, 'The Network of Global Corporate Control', Arxiv.org, 19 September 2011: https://arxiv.org/PS_cache/arxiv/pdf/1107/1107.5728v2.pdf.
12 Nicholas Shaxson, 'Tackling Tax Havens', International Monetary Fund, September 2019: www.imf.org/en/Publications/fandd/issues/2019/09/tackling-global-tax-havens-shaxon.
13 Just one example is the exploitive and damaging nature of the international 'Big Chocolate' business: two-thirds of cacao comes from the Ivory Coast and Ghana, where rainforest has been lost to cacao production, ecological diversity has been diminished, and labour including child labour – an estimated 1.5 million children – earns as little as $1 a day. Rowan Jacobsen, *Wild Chocolate: Across the Americas in Search of Cacao's Soul* (Bloomsbury, 2024).

NOTES

14 Terrence McCoy and Júlia Ledur, 'How Americans' Love of Beef Is Helping to Destroy the Amazon Rainforest', *Washington Post*, 29 April 2022: www.washingtonpost.com/world/interactive/2022/amazon-beef-deforestation-brazil/.

15 Kay, *Corporation*.

16 Kalyeena Makortoff and Anna Isaac, 'How Private Equity Convinced Labour to Go Easy on Its Multimillion Pound Tax Perk', *Guardian*, 31 October 2024: www.theguardian.com/business/2024/oct/31/how-private-equity-convinced-labour-to-go-easy-on-its-multimillion-pound-tax-perk.

17 Tax Justice UK: https://taxjustice.uk.

18 Filipe Pacheco and Diana Li, 'Trump Win Sparks Record $64 Billion Gain for World's 10 Richest People', *Bloomberg*, 7 November 2024: www.bloomberg.com/news/articles/2024-11-07/trump-s-election-win-supercharges-net-worth-of-worlds-richest-by-64-billion; Jordan Valinsky, 'The World's 10 Richest People Got a Record $64 Billion Richer from Trump's Reelection', CNN, 7 November 2024: https://edition.cnn.com/2024/11/07/investing/billionaires-net-worth-trump-win/index.html.

19 Valinsky, 'World's 10 Richest People'.

20 Daniela Ginzburg, 'Multinational Corporations Undermining Democracy, Report Says', *Ynet News*, 24 September 2024: www.ynetnews.com/business/article/skpihnl0r. The ITUC represents nearly 200 million workers in 169 countries.

21 The media in October and November 2024 was full of reports of both. See e.g. Derek Robertson, 'Elon Musk Goes All-in for Trump', *Politico*, 11 May 2024: www.politico.com/news/2024/11/05/elon-musk-trump-twitter-x-election-00187467; Katie

Robertson and Benjamin Mullin, 'Jeff Bezos Defends Decision to End *Washington Post* Endorsements', *Washington Post*, 28 October 2024: www.nytimes.com/2024/10/28/business/media/washington-post-endorsement-editorial-board.html.

22 News media in the UK in December 2024 reported that Elon Musk was planning to give $100 million to Nigel Farage's far-right Reform Party in the UK in an effort to put it into power at the next available occurrence of a general election. See e.g. William Mata, 'Elon Musk Tipped to Give $100m to Nigel Farage in Move to Shake up British Politics', *London Evening Standard*, 1 December 2024: www.standard.co.uk/news/uk/elon-musk-nigel-farage-donald-trump-reform-uk-b1197417.html.

23 Ginzburg, 'Multinational Corporations'.

24 This was the result of tireless efforts by *Observer* journalist Carole Cadwalladr. Carole Cadwalladr, as told to Lee Glendinning, 'Exposing Cambridge Analytica: "It's Been Exhausting, Exhilarating, and Slightly Terrifying"', *Guardian*, 29 September 2018: www.theguardian.com/membership/2018/sep/29/cambridge-analytica-cadwalladr-observer-facebook-zuckerberg-wylie. The involvement of Meta (as it was later renamed) was revealed by whistle-blower Christopher Wylie.

25 See A.C. Grayling, *For the Good of the World* (Oneworld, 2022) on the efforts of pro-fossil fuel industries to distract and divert from climate change issues.

26 A.C. Grayling, *Discriminations: Achieving Peace in the Culture Wars* (Oneworld, 2025).

27 Freedom House: https://freedomhouse.org; see the Freedom House webinar, 'The Business of Freedom: How Markets Can

NOTES

Support Democracy and Counter Authoritarianism', YouTube, 16 November 2022, www.youtube.com/watch?v=dPb_A0BIq48, which specifically addresses the value of upholding democratic values and human rights to national and transnational business.

28 William Rees-Mogg and James Dale Davidson, *The Sovereign Individual* (Touchstone, 1997).

29 'Freedom in the World Index 2024', Freedom House: https://freedomhouse.org/report/freedom-world.

30 See, for example, Daniel Boffey, 'How Will Recent and Future Legislation Affect the Right to Protest in the UK?', *Guardian*, 13 November 2023: www.theguardian.com/world/2023/nov/13/how-will-recent-and-future-legislation-affect-the-right-to-protest-in-the-uk.

31 Amnesty International's report on Hungary 2023: www.amnesty.org/en/location/europe-and-central-asia/western-central-and-south-eastern-europe/hungary/report-hungary/.

32 Amnesty International's report on India 2023: www.amnesty.org/en/location/asia-and-the-pacific/south-asia/india/report-india/.

33 Human Rights Watch's report on Myanmar 2022: www.hrw.org/world-report/2023/country-chapters/myanmar.

34 Tragically, alas, a reading of Simon Sebag-Montefiore's *Jerusalem* (Weidenfeld & Nicolson, 2011) shows that the events in Israel and Gaza in 2023–5 are 'normal' for the region which, for three thousand years, as a crossroad between empires and the site of typically vicious and explosive interreligious and sectarian rivalries, has weltered in blood throughout its appalling history.

35 The founder of Alibaba in China, Jack Ma, might serve as an example; after criticising government regulators he suffered what appears to be a backlash from them, losing half his wealth and having to step down from his position. An intended IPO by Ant (formerly Ant Financial), part-owned by Alibaba, was halted by the Chinese government, and a heavy general crackdown on private enterprise followed. See Michelle Toh, 'Jack Ma Loses Half His Wealth after Criticizing Chinese Regulators', CNN, 12 July 2023: https://edition.cnn.com/2023/07/12/business/china-jack-ma-wealth-drop-intl-hnk/index.html.

36 Mordecai Kurz, 'How Capitalism Became a Threat to Democracy', *Project Syndicate*, 15 March 2024: www.project-syndicate.org/onpoint/how-capitalism-became-a-threat-to-democracy-by-mordecai-kurz-2024-03. See also Kurz, *The Market Power of Technology* (Columbia University Press, 2023).

37 Kurz, 'How Capitalism Became a Threat'.

38 Ibid.

39 Ibid.

40 Michael Bauer, 'Populist Governments as a Threat from within the State', *The Loop*: https://theloop.ecpr.eu/populist-governments-as-a-threat-from-within-the-state/.

41 See Peter Morris, 'The North East's Biggest Scandal for 50 Years', *North East Bylines*, 15 February 2024: https://northeastbylines.co.uk/region/teesside/the-north-easts-biggest-scandal-for-50-years/.

42 Ann Moody, 'Special Economic Zones in the UK – Ideology over Public Interest?', *Yorkshire Bylines*, 14 January 2024: https://york-

shirebylines.co.uk/news/home-affairs/special-economic-zones-in-the-uk-ideology-over-public-interest/.
43 See Sarah Moser, 'Analysing a Private City', *Urban Studies*, Vol. 61, May 2024.
44 Moody, 'Special Economic Zones'.
45 Ibid.
46 Ibid.
47 Ibid.
48 'Peter Thiel', Wikipedia: https://en.wikipedia.org/wiki/Peter_Thiel.
49 Dan Milmo, 'Palantir's Peter Thiel: NHS is a Natural Target for Outspoken Tech Billionaire', *Guardian*, 21 November 2023: www.theguardian.com/technology/2023/nov/21/palantir-peter-thiel-nhs-natural-target-outspoken-tech-billionaire.
50 Próspera Inc.'s website: www.prospera.co/en.
51 'Billionaires are Suing the Honduran Government for Blocking Their Profit-Making Scheme', *Jacobin*, 27 November 2023: https://jacobin.com/2023/11/honduras-international-law-isds-thiel-prospera-free-market-neocolonialism; Business and Human Rights Resource Centre report, 19 July 2023: www.business-humanrights.org/en/latest-news/honduras-threatens-withdrawal-from-investment-dispute-tribunal-over-11-billion-claim-by-us-firm-prospera/.
52 Derek Offord, *Ayn Rand and the Russian Intelligentsia: The Origins of an Icon of the American Right* (Bloomsbury, 2022).
53 Christopher Hitchens, 'Greenspan Shrugged', *Vanity Fair*, 6 December 2000: https://www.vanityfair.com/culture/2000/12/hitchens-200012. The article demonstrates how Greenspan's

'official record shows how Washington can compromise even the most passionate of principles' – a point that cuts both ways.

54 See Judith Niechcial, 'The NHS Is Being Systematically Dismantled by Privatisation', *We Own It*, 11 June 2020: https://weownit.org.uk/blog/nhs-being-systematically-dismantled-privatisation.

55 A classic statement of the view and its sources is given in a 2017 essay by a leading proponent of it, Nick Land, in his 'A Quick and Dirty Introduction to Accelerationism', 25 May 2017: www.scribd.com/document/639952390/Untitled.

56 Sophie Alexander and Dana Hull, 'Elon Wants You to Have More Babies', *Bloomberg Businessweek*, 21 June 2024: www.bloomberg.com/features/2024-elon-musk-population-collapse-baby-push/.

57 Kyle Wiggers, 'Elon Musk Reportedly Donated $10 Million to a Fertility Research Project', *Techcrunch*, 16 August 2023: https://techcrunch.com/2023/08/16/elon-musk-reportedly-donated-10-million-to-a-fertility-research-project/.

58 'Eugenics', *History*, 28 October 2019.

59 Lisa Ko, 'Unwanted Sterilization and Eugenics Programs in the United States', *Independent Lens*, PBS, 29 January 2016: www.pbs.org/independentlens/blog/unwanted-sterilization-and-eugenics-programs-in-the-united-states/.

60 From transcript of NPR broadcast on eugenics in the US. 'The Supreme Court Ruling that Led to 70,000 Forced Sterilizations', *Fresh Air*, NPR, 7 March 2016: www.npr.org/sections/health-shots/2016/03/07/469478098/the-supreme-court-ruling-that-led-to-70-000-forced-sterilizations.

61 Sarah Wise's *The Undesirables* (Oneworld, 2024) shows how close the UK came to this in the early twentieth century.

NOTES

62 Should any more evidence be required to support the contention that masked international libertarian influence is active and highly influential in politics and government, Peter Geoghegan's 'The "Dark Money" Linking Trump and the British Right' will more than suffice. Peter Geoghegan, 'The "Dark Money" Linking Trump and the British Right', *Prospect*, 8 November 2024: www.prospectmagazine.co.uk/politics/68486/dark-money-donald-trump-british-right-farage.

63 David Marchese, 'The Interview: Curtis Yarvin Says Democracy Is Done. Powerful Conservatives Are Listening', *New York Times* magazine, 18 January 2025: www.nytimes.com/2025/01/18/magazine/curtis-yarvin-interview.html See also Ava Kofman on Yarvin, 'Trumpworld's Court Philosopher', *New Yorker*, 2 June 2025: https://www.newyorker.com/newsletter/the-daily/trumpworlds-court-philosopher.

64 Julian E. Zelizer, *Burning Down the House: Newt Gingrich, the Fall of the Speaker, and the Rise of the New Republican Party* (Penguin, 2020).

65 Michael Tomsky, 'Democrats: This Is War. Isn't it Time You Acted Like It?', *New Republic*, 10 February 2025.

66 Paul Rogers, 'Our Global Culture of War Means Guaranteed Profits for the Arms Industry', openDemocracy, 23 June 2023: www.opendemocracy.net/en/arms-industry-shareholder-capitalism-perfect-war-syria-iraq-ukraine/.

67 Stockholm International Peace Research Institute: www.sipri.org.

68 Small Arms Survey's report on global firearms holdings, 2018: www.smallarmssurvey.org/database/global-firearms-holdings.

69 A.C. Grayling, *War: An Enquiry* (Yale University Press, 2016).

70 Jordi Calvo Rufanges, 'No Business without Enemies: War and the Arms Trade', *Transnational Institute Longreads*, May 2021: https://longreads.tni.org/stateofpower/no-business-without-enemies-war-and-the-arms-trade.

71 In an *Observer* article of 10 November 2024 the indomitable Carole Cadwalladr, reviewing how social media has been used since 2015 to undermine democracy – about which she consistently warned following its manipulations to influence the Brexit referendum in the UK and the first election of Trump to the White House – concluded: 'this is oligarchy now. This is the fusion of state and commercial power in a ruling elite … The chaos of Russia in the 90s is the template; billions will be made, people will die, crimes will be committed.' Carole Cadwalladr, 'A New Era Dawns. America's Tech Bros Now Strut Their Stuff in the Corridors of Power', *Observer*, 10 November 2024: www.theguardian.com/commentisfree/2024/nov/11/a-new-era-dawns-americas-tech-bros-now-strut-their-stuff-in-the-corridors-of-power.

72 An instructive observation of the culture of aspects of big business is provided by Sarah Wynn-Williams in *Careless People* (Macmillan, 2025).

3 The Alternative Model: Turning to Authoritarianism

1 Drew DeSilver, 'More Countries Are Now Democratic than at Any Point since World War Two', World Economic Forum, 11 December 2017: www.weforum.org/stories/2017/12/more-

countries-are-now-democratic-than-at-any-point-since-world-war-two/.
2 Ibid.
3 Steven Levitsky and Daniel Ziblatt, *Tyranny of the Minority* (Viking, 2023).
4 Organization of American States, *Charter of the Organization of American States* (1948–93), art. 1.
5 'International Election Observation', Electoral Knowledge Network: https://aceproject.org/ace-en/focus/international-election-observation/default.
6 Susan D. Hyde, *The Pseudo-Democrat's Dilemma* (Cornell University Press, 2011): https://library.oapen.org/bitstream/id/336e54ca-695d-4594-974b-5aae6a3f091f/626997.pdf.
7 Ibid.
8 Ibid.
9 The discrepancy between the Pew and *Economist* indexes, a minor one, is explained by the slightly differing criteria used.
10 See David Vine, 'How US Military Bases Back Dictators, Autocrats, and Military Regimes', *HuffPost*, 16 May 2017: www.huffpost.com/entry/how-us-military-bases-back-dictators-autocrats-and-military-regimes_b_591b229ae4b05dd15f0ba8e6. See also Dina Smeltz and Emily Sullivan, 'Most Americans Willing to Work with Autocrats to Protect the US', Chicago Council on Global Affairs, 17 October 2022: https://globalaffairs.org/research/public-opinion-survey/most-americans-willing-work-autocrats-protect-us.
11 'Human Rights-Based Approach', UN Sustainable Development Group: https://unsdg.un.org/2030-agenda/universal-values/human-rights-based-approach#:~:text=The%20human%20

rights%2Dbased%20approach,promoting%20and%20protecting%20human%20rights.

12 Anne Applebaum, *Autocracy Inc. The Dictators who Want to Run the World* (Doubleday, 2024).

13 Ruth Ben-Ghiat, *Strongmen: How They Rise, Why They Succeed, How They Fall* (Profile, 2020).

14 Committee on Political Affairs and Democracy, 'The Challenge of Far-Right Ideology to Democracy and Human Rights in Europe', Parliamentary Assembly, Council of Europe: https://rm.coe.int/the-challenge-of-far-right-ideology-to-democracy-and-human-rights-in-e/1680ac86d0.

15 Tyler Cowen, 'China's Success Explains Authoritarianism's Allure', *Bloomberg*, 3 April 2017: www.bloomberg.com/view/articles/2017-04-03/china-s-success-explains-authoritarianisms-allure.

16 'China in the World', Ford Foundation: www.fordfoundation.org/our-work-around-the-world/china/china-in-the-world/. See also David Shambaugh, *China and the World* (Oxford University Press, 2020).

17 Nico Hines, 'Inside Bannon's Plan to Hijack Europe for the Far-Right', *Daily Beast*, 20 July 2018: www.thedailybeast.com/inside-bannons-plan-to-hijack-europe-for-the-far-right; 'The Movement: How Steve Bannon Is Spreading Populist Trump-Style Politics across Europe', *Independent*, 27 September 2018: www.independent.co.uk/news/long_reads/steve-bannon-the-movement-europe-populist-nationalism-trump-a8557156.html.

18 Open Society Foundations' website: www.opensocietyfoundations.org/.

NOTES

19 See Maya Goodfellow, 'How Worried Should We Be about Steve Bannon's "Movement"?', *Al Jazeera*, 10 August 2018: www.aljazeera.com/opinions/2018/8/10/how-worried-should-we-be-about-steve-bannons-movement/.

20 A.C. Grayling, 'Chinese Philosophy', in *The History of Philosophy* (Penguin Books, 2019).

21 'The Nuremberg Race Laws', United States Holocaust Memorial Museum's *Holocaust Encyclopedia*: https://encyclopedia.ushmm.org/content/en/article/the-nuremberg-race-laws.

22 An excellent brief survey of the apartheid laws of South Africa is given on Britannica: www.britannica.com/topic/apartheid.

23 Note that the phrase 'a rule of law' meaning 'a legal rule', e.g. about having to register your motor vehicle or notifying the authorities of a birth or death in the family, is not at issue here; '*the* rule of law' is sometimes written 'The Rule of Law' with capital letters to make this clear.

24 'Not harming others' both recalls John Stuart Mill's 'harm principle' (that the only justification the state can have to interfere with anyone is if what they do harms others) and the question of what constitutes 'harm' – on the spectrum from murder to hurting someone's feelings there are plenty of obvious candidates and (especially lately) a number of new alleged candidates, but it is not outwith the wit of human beings to identify which ones are plausible.

25 Timothy Snyder, *On Tyranny* (Penguin, 2017).

26 A telling depiction of what such life is like is given by the film *The Lives of Others* about life in East Berlin before the Wall came down in 1989. A chilling prediction is offered by *2073*, a film by

Asif Kapadia; see the trailer at www.youtube.com/watch?v=f02lF_iJ1FA.

27 Shoshana Zuboff, *The Age of Surveillance Capitalism* (Profile Books, 2019).

An example, both amusing and troubling, is the experience of a New York friend of mine: he made an online booking for an appointment at a medical clinic in the city, and in the following days was bombarded with advertisements for funeral services. This was because information about him, his age and occupation, the services offered by the clinic, and enough details about other such appointments in his online history, was available for an actuarial algorithm to identify him as a suitable target for the advertisements. The thought that AI, feeding on the masses of data points accumulated about each of us individually, can tell us that we are about to die, when our doctors are more cautious in their prognoses and making efforts to keep us alive, is an uncomfortable one.

28 Charlie Savage and Michael Gold, 'Trump Confirms Plans to Use the Military to Assist in Mass Deportations', *New York Times*, 18 November 2024: www.nytimes.com/2024/11/18/us/politics/trump-military-mass-deportation.html.

29 Ben-Ghiat, *Strongmen*; Applebaum, *Autocracy, Inc.*

30 Applebaum, *Autocracy, Inc.*

31 BRIC stands for Brazil, Russia, India and China. BRICs+ includes South Africa, Egypt, Iran, the United Arab Emirates and Ethiopia, along with the original four.

32 Applebaum, *Autocracy, Inc.*

33 Ibid.

NOTES

34 See Carole Cadwalladr, 'Google, Democracy and the Truth about Internet Search', *Guardian*, 4 December 2016: www.theguardian.com/technology/2016/dec/04/google-democracy-truth-internet-search-facebook.

35 Applebaum, *Autocracy, Inc.*

36 Britain maintained global domination through a mixture of 'informal' as well as actual empire until the 1880s 'Scramble for Africa' impelled it into converting informal to formal empire in the interior of the African continent; see the chapter in my *Who Owns the Moon?* (Oneworld, 2024) on the African colonisation scramble where the 'informal empire' and 'spheres of interest' doctrines are discussed.

37 Quoted in ibid.

38 Larry Diamond, 'The Fight Against Autocracy Needs a New Playbook', *Foreign Affairs*, November–December 2024.

39 Ibid.

40 Ibid.

41 Ibid.

42 Larry M. Bartels, 'The Populist Phantom: Threats to Democracy Start at the Top', *Foreign Affairs*, November–December 2024.

   It should be added that absolute monarchies such as the United Arab Emirates and Saudi Arabia provide other examples of authoritarian states, an individual or royal family in effect owning the state and disposing of all that happens within it. In these cases the power is inherited and is sustained by tradition. They are functionally indistinguishable from any authoritarian arrangement. It is unlikely that any state currently transitioning towards authoritarianism would aim at becoming (or restoring) an absolute monarchy in form and name, despite *de facto* becoming or already being one.

43 The *New York Times* kept a running list of Trump's initiatives from soon after his inauguration in January 2025 and can be consulted in that source (e.g. www.nytimes.com/interactive/2025/us/trump-agenda-2025.html).

44 Trump banning Associated Press and Reuters from White House press briefings because they refuse to uncritically relay falsehoods uttered at the podium, while inviting social media 'influencers' who support his agenda in their place, and Mark Zuckerberg's abolition of fact controls on his social media platforms, are staring examples.

45 See Amy Slipowitz and Mina Loldj, 'Silenced in Prison, Repressed Outside: Damage Done by Political Imprisonment and "Civil Death"', Freedom House, 25 January 2024: https://freedomhouse.org/article/silenced-prison-repressed-outside-damage-done-political-imprisonment-and-civil-death; A.S. Matthews, 'Political Purges and Their Importance for Dictators', *The Loop*, European Consortium for Political Research, 2 September 2022: https://theloop.ecpr.eu/political-purges-and-their-importance-for-dictators/. In the US the murder of Minnesota Democrat state congresswoman Melissa Hortman and her husband Mark on 13 June 2025 is an instance of a Trump supporter, inflamed by the violent rhetoric of the MAGA-sphere and Trump himself, acting on the logic of that rhetoric. Minnesota State Senator John A. Hoffman, a fellow Democrat, and his wife Yvette were also, but non-fatally, attacked by the gunman. The shootings occurred on the night before the huge 'No Kings' demonstrations against Trump on Saturday 14 June 2025.

46 A salutary experience is provided by watching the film *2073*.

47 See the Free Press panel discussion with Maria Ressa et al.: Free Press, 'Defeating Authoritarianism: How People and Media Can Stand Up for Freedom Now', YouTube, 27 February 2025, www.youtube.com/watch?v=OOIOSFtHKbQ; Maria Ressa, *How to Stand Up to a Dictator* (Random House, 2022).

Standing up to dictators works: on 11 March 2025 the *New York Times* reported that Rodrigo Duterte, the Philippine ex-President against whom Maria Ressa campaigned, was arrested in Manila on an International Criminal Court warrant accusing him of crimes against humanity. Sui-Lee Wee and Camille Elemia, 'Rodrigo Duterte, Philippine Ex-President, Is Arrested on ICC Warrant', *New York Times*, 10 March 2025: https://www.nytimes.com/2025/03/10/world/asia/icc-philippines-rodrigo-duterte.html.

4 Interference Undermining Democracy

1 In A.C. Grayling, *Liberty in the Age of Terror* (Bloomsbury, 2009), I argued that by restricting civil liberties in hopes of deterring or catching terrorists, democracies were doing what the terrorists wished to achieve: to degrade the societies they attacked, and make them more like the illiberal (in their case theocratic) regimes whose ideologies they espoused. I quoted Benjamin Franklin: 'Those who would exchange liberty for security deserve neither'. A group of home affairs ministers in the European Union, then including the UK, jointly published an essay stating that the first duty of government was to protect the safety of their citizens; I argued that although this was indeed a high responsibility, their true first duty was to protect the liberties of citizens.

2   See Grayling, *Discriminations*.
3   Ibid.
4   Jonathan Haidt, 'Yes, Social Media Really Is Undermining Democracy', *The Atlantic*, 28 July 2022: www.theatlantic.com/ideas/archive/2022/07/social-media-harm-facebook-meta-response/670975/.
5   Ibid.
6   Ibid.
7   Juan Pablo Cardenal, a commentator on Chinese influence in Latin America, Jacek Kucharczyk, president of the Polish think tank IPA, Grigorij Mesežnikov, president of the IVO in Slovakia, and Gabriela Pleschová of the Institute of International Relations in Bratislava (both IPA and IVO stand for 'Institute of Public Affairs' in their respective countries); introductory chapter of *Sharp Power: Rising Authoritarian Influence* by Christopher Walker and Jessica Ludwig, National Endowment for Democracy, 5 December 2017: www.ned.org/sharp-power-rising-authoritarian-influence-forum-report/.
8   Ibid.
9   Ibid.
10 Ibid.
11 Ibid.
12 Sam Cabral, 'US Accuses Russia of 2024 Election Interference', BBC, 4 September 2024: www.bbc.com/news/articles/c8rx28v1vpro.
13 Peter Walker, 'Party Funding Linked to Russia – How Much Have Tories Benefitted?', *Guardian*, 23 February 2022: www.theguardian.com/politics/2022/feb/23/oligarchs-funding-tories.
14 T.J. Coles, 'The Conservatives Have a Long History of Taking Money from Russia', *Byline Times*, 1 March 2022: https://bylinetimes.

NOTES

com/2022/03/01/the-conservatives-have-a-long-history-of-taking-money-from-russia/.

15 Théo Prouvost, 'Moldovan Dreams and Georgian Nightmares: Putin Meddles in European "Swing States"', *Byline Times*, 4 November 2024: https://bylinetimes.com/2024/11/04/moldovan-dreams-and-georgian-nightmares-putin-meddles-in-european-swing-states/.

16 '89up Releases Report on Russian Influence in the EU Referendum', 89up, 23 February 2018: https://89up.org/russia-report; Haroon Siddique, 'Cadwalladr Reports on Arron Banks' Russian Links', *Guardian*, 21 January 2022: www.theguardian.com/world/2022/jan/21/cadwalladr-reports-on-arron-banks-russia-links-of-huge-public-interest-court-hears (Banks was a significant donor to the 'Leave' campaign).

17 Rachel Ellehuus and Donatienne Ruy, 'Did Russia Influence Brexit?', Center for Strategic and International Studies, 21 July 2020: www.csis.org/blogs/brexit-bits-bobs-and-blogs/did-russia-influence-brexit.

18 Ibid.

19 Lee Edwards, 'Confucian Institutes: China's Trojan Horse', Heritage Foundation, 27 May 2021: www.heritage.org/homeland-security/commentary/confucius-institutes-chinas-trojan-horse.

20 'Confucius Institutes: The Growth of China's Controversial Cultural Branch', BBC, 7 September 2019: www.bbc.com/news/world-asia-china-49511231.

21 Anthony Kleven, 'Belt and Road: Colonialism with Chinese Characteristics', *The Interpreter*, Lowy Institute: www.lowyinstitute.org/the-interpreter/belt-road-colonialism-chinese-characteristics.

22 Ibid.
23 Ibid.
24 Ibid.
25 Witness Trump's sidelining of the US's NATO allies in the February 2025 'Ukraine peace talks' between the US and Russia alone, conducted by telephone conversation between Trump and Putin and the US–Russia foreign affairs officials meeting in Saudi Arabia, both widely reported in the media.
26 'Joint Statement of the Russian Federation and the People's Republic of China on the International Relations Entering a New Era and the Global Sustainable Development', 4 February 2022: www.en.kremlin.ru/supplement/5770.
27 Applebaum, *Autocracy, Inc.*, and her interview at the Bush Institute, 15 November 2024: www.bushcenter.org/publications/book-review-applebaum-discusses-authoritarian-threat-to-democracies-in-autocracy-inc.
28 Applebaum, *Autocracy, Inc.*
29 Maria Snegovaya, 'Why Russia's Democracy Never Began', *Journal of Democracy*, Vol. 34, No. 3, July 2023: www.journalofdemocracy.org/articles/why-russias-democracy-never-began/.
30 Ibid.
31 Ibid.
32 Ibid.
33 Georgi Kantchev and Warren P. Strobel, 'How Russia's "Info Warrior" Hackers Let Kremlin Play Geopolitics on the Cheap', *Wall Street Journal*, 2 January 2021.
34 Nearly two thousand properties in London are owned by Russian nationals; see Ella Jessel, 'Revealed: The True Scale of Russian-

NOTES

Owned Property in London Is Far Greater than Official Records Show', *Standard*, 11 May 2022: www.standard.co.uk/homesand-property/property-news/revealed-true-scale-russian-owned-property-in-london-b995498.html.

'At a minimum, from cases reported in the last five years, more than $2.3 billion has been laundered through US real estate, including millions more through other alternative assets, like art, jewellery and yachts, according to a report in August by Global Financial Integrity, a nonprofit group that researches illicit money flows.' See Heidi Przybyla and Christine Haughney, 'Russian Money Flows through US Real Estate', *NBC News*, 2 March 2022: www.nbcnews.com/business/real-estate/russian-money-flows-us-real-estate-rcna17723.

35 This is in addition to methods similar to Russia's direct interventions technologically and by lobbying and subversion abroad; see for example the report on 14 March 2025 in the Euractiv newsletter *The Capitals:* 'The EU woke up yesterday morning to the news that Belgian police are investigating Huawei for possible bribery of EU lawmakers – but it was already clear that the Chinese tech giant likes to throw money around. Huawei funds several influential policy associations in Brussels, according to its entry on the EU's Transparency Register, where companies report their lobbying activities'; https://www.euractiv.com/section/politics/news/huaweis-tentacles-in-brussels/.

36 J.R. Biden, 'Why America Must Lead Again: Rescuing US Foreign Policy after Trump', *Foreign Affairs*, 23 January 2020: www.foreignaffairs.com/articles/united-states/2020-01-23/why-america-must-lead-again.

37 Summit for Democracy 2021, United States Department of State: https://2021-2025.state.gov/summit-for-democracy-2021/.
38 X. Deng, 'An Undemocratic "Summit for Democracy"', *China Daily*, 10 December 2021: https://global.chinadaily.com.cn/a/202112/10/WS61b2c2ffa310cdd39bc7a987.html.
39 K. Bradsher and S.L. Myers, 'Ahead of Biden's Democracy Summit, China Says: We're Also a Democracy', *New York Times*, 7 December 2021: www.nytimes.com/2021/12/07/world/asia/china-biden-democracy-summit.html; M. Leonard, 'Xi Jinping's Idea of World Order', European Council on Foreign Relations, 5 April 2023: https://ecfr.eu/article/xi-jinpings-idea-of-world-order/.
40 Young Chul Cho, 'China's Promoting of Authoritarian-Westphalian Democracy and its Implications for the Liberal International Order', *Issues and Studies*, Vol. 60, No. 3, 2024: https://www.worldscientific.com/doi/10.1142/S1013251124500115?srsltid=.

Cho quotes extensively from the documents of China's Ministry of Foreign Affairs and State Council Information Office, and these sources are utilised here via his study.
41 Ibid.
42 Ibid., quoting J. Ai, 'Washington Not World's "Beacon of Democracy"', *Global Times*, 16 September 2023: www.globaltimes.cn/page/201909/1164625.shtml.

The *Global Times* is an organ of the Chinese Communist Party published by the Beijing *People's Daily* (*Renmin Ribao*).
43 Ibid., quoting Ministry of Foreign Affairs of the People's Republic of China and *The State of Democracy in the United States: 2022*, State Council Information Office of the People's Republic of China.

NOTES

44 'China: Democracy that Works', State Council Information Office of the People's Republic of China, *Chinhua Net*, 4 December 2021: www.news.cn/english/2021-12/04/c_1310351231.htm.
45 Cho, 'China's Promoting'.
46 Ministry of Foreign Affairs of the People's Republic of China, 2021, quoted in Cho, 'China's Promoting'.
47 Cho, 'China's Promoting'.
48 Quoted in ibid.
49 'Dictator' derives etymologically from *dico* 'to speak' via *dicto* to 'dictate' or 'prescribe'.
50 'China: Democracy that Works'.
51 Cho, 'China's Promoting'.
52 'Aggressiveness of US Democracy Derived from Hegemony, Bullying and Domineering', 11 February 2023, *Global Times*: www.globaltimes.cn/ page/202302/1285239.shtml, quoted in Cho, 'China's Promoting'.
53 Ministry of Foreign Affairs of the People's Republic of China, 2021, quoted in Cho, 'China's Promoting'.
54 Xi Jinping, *China Daily*, 16 October 2022: www.chinadaily.com.cn/a/202 210/16/WS634b8a6da310fd2b29e7cc6c.html.
55 Amnesty International's China report, 2023: www.amnesty.org/en/location/asia-and-the-pacific/east-asia/china/report-china/.
56 *UN Universal Periodic Review of China. Mid-term Report*, The Rights Practice, November 2021: www.ohchr.org/sites/default/files/2021-11/TheRightsPractice_UPR_of_China_Mid-term_Report_November2021.pdf.
57 The UK organisation was 'June Fourth'. Harry Wu, who spent nineteen years in a Chinese labour camp ('laogai', the Chinese

gulag) and after escaping China founded the Laogai Research Foundation in the US, was a colleague in the endeavour; his book *Bitter Winds* (Jossey-Bass, 1994) is an excoriating account of life under the regime. The Chinese friend and colleague with whom I co-authored *The Long March to the Fourth of June* (Duckworth, 1989) under the joint pseudonym of 'Li Xiao Jun' (on the history of the CCP) has spent several terms in prison.

58 Koh Ewe and Phoebe Kong, 'Hong Kong Jails 45 Pro-Democracy Campaigners for Subversion', BBC, 18 November 2024: www.bbc.com/news/articles/cx2l4eynl4zo.

59 Edward Cho and Dorothy Kam, 'Hong Kong "Patriots Only" Election Falls Flat with Record Low Turnout', *Reuters*, 11 December 2023: www.reuters.com/world/china/hong-kong-patriots-only-election-falls-flat-with-record-low-turnout-2023-12-11/.

60 Jane Ho and Yue Wang, 'China's 100 Richest', *Forbes*, 6 November 2024: www.forbes.com/lists/china-billionaires/; 'Hurun China Rich List', Hurun Research Institute, 29 October 2024: www.hurun.net/en-us/info/detail?num=8S9MBRWXLAT6.

61 'Li Xiao Jun', *Long March*.

62 This is an inference naturally drawn from the support for Trump of billionaires such as Elon Musk, Peter Thiel and Jeff Bezos. The influence of Rupert Murdoch – owner of Fox News and other broadcast media outlets, the *Wall Street Journal* and a stable of right-wing British and Australian newspapers – is a long-recognised problem.

63 Francis Fukuyama, Barak Richman and Ashish Goel, 'How to Save Democracy from Technology: Ending Big Tech's Information Monopoly', *Foreign Affairs*, January–February 2021, first

NOTES

published online 24 November 2020: www.foreignaffairs.com/articles/united-states/2020-11-24/fukuyama-how-save-democracy-technology.

64 The Network Enforcement Act 2017 (*Gesetz zur Verbesserung der Rechtsdurchsetzung in sozialen Netzwerken*, colloquially known as the 'NetzDG' and 'Facebook Act'). Critics accused it of curtailing freedom of expression; this is of course the chief problem with legal control of internet content. In the US invocation of First Amendment rights make regulation even more difficult.

65 Fukuyama et al., 'How to Save Democracy'.

66 Ibid.

67 Ibid.

68 Ibid.

69 Ibid.

70 Grayling, *Discriminations*.

71 The Council of Europe is not to be confused with the European Union. It is a body of forty-six member states, of which all twenty-seven states of the EU are members. It is the home of the European Court of Human Rights and the Council of Europe Development Bank (which has an exclusively social mandate) and was founded in London on 5 May 1949.

72 Committee on Political Affairs and Democracy, 'Challenge of Far-Right Ideology'.

73 Ibid., §1.6.

74 Ibid., §1.9.

75 Ibid., §1.10.

76 Ibid., §1.13.

77 Ibid., §1.16.

78 Ibid., §1.19.

79 Ibid., §3.2–3.
80 Ibid., §3.3.32.
81 It is made the more spectacular by the fact that the US is never usually shy about putting people behind bars; it imprisons more people than anywhere else in the world – with five per cent of the world's population, the US has twenty-five per cent of the world's prisoners (a disproportionate number of them people of colour). This figure almost certainly omits those held without formal trial in China and Russia. China ranks second to the US in its acknowledged prison population, but it occupies first place in Asia, holding four times as many in jail as the region's next most energetic incarcerator, India. See Statista Research Department, 'Crime and Penitentiary System in China – Statistics & Facts', *Statista*, 20 December 2023: www.statista.com/topics/2253/crime-and-penitentiary-system-in-china/#:~:text=In%20recent%20years%2C%20presumably%20around,the%20runner%2Dup%2C%20India.
82 Committee on Political Affairs and Democracy, 'Challenge of Far-Right Ideology', §5.43.
83 Ibid., §5.53.
84 These proposals, here summarised generally, are made out in detail in §5 *passim*; see Appendix II.

5 Restoring Democracy

1 See Grayling, *Democracy*, and *The Good State*.
2 Grayling, *Towards the Light*.

NOTES

3   I shall cite two examples to their shame: Keir Starmer and David Lammy, senior members of a party of which I've several times been a member (this to imply the equal number of times I've resigned from it in dismay or disgust). At time of writing Sir Keir Starmer is the Prime Minister of the United Kingdom. In the 2016 Brexit referendum campaign he opposed Brexit, argued in favour of a second referendum, and afterwards argued that Single Market membership and freedom of movement for all in Europe, including the UK, is a necessary good. On becoming Prime Minister he flipped 180 degrees to supporting the 'hard Brexit' clumsily effected by Boris Johnson during the latter's disastrous premiership, refused to explain why, and despite rhetoric about 'resetting relations' with Europe emphatically ruled out reversing Brexit.

David Lammy, at time of writing Foreign Secretary of the United Kingdom, made a famously passionate and eloquent speech in the House of Commons in January 2019 in opposition to Brexit, calling it 'a con, a swindle, fraud'; now at time of writing he toes the 'no reversing Brexit' line. If he believed what he said in his famous speech – and the facts have borne him out – it is incomprehensible how so complete a volte-face is anything but 'principle melting before expediency', though it is a mystery to the majority of the British population (a consistent ± 60 per cent have supported rejoining the EU for years before and at this writing) what the expediency is, apart from electoral calculations designed to keep the Labour Party in government even though Brexit is so contrary to the country's interests. This is because of the exaggerated effects in the British system of a change of voting by a relatively small number of voters in a relatively small number of constituencies; a change of a couple of percentage points can rocket a party's seats in Parliament from an impotent minority to a massive majority. Thus, party self-interest kowtowing to a small number of voters holds the country hostage.

For US readers an even more striking example is the performance of Republican politicians who, before Trump's re-election, had few good things to say about him – his now Vice-President actually likened him to Hitler – is craven beyond nauseating. The measure of the combination of fear and party partisanship that motivates them to behave in so dishonest and spineless a manner is the measure of the threat to American democracy itself.

4   Mikhail Bakunin, *Statism and Anarchy* (1873; Cambridge University Press, 1970).
5   Tim Lau, 'Citizens United Explained', Brennan Center for Justice, 12 December 2019: www.brennancenter.org/our-work/research-reports/citizens-united-explained.
6   Grayling, *Democracy and Its Crisis*.
7   Judit Bayer, 'Policies and Measures to Counter Disinformation in Germany', Heinrich Böll Stiftung, 13 October 2021: https://eu.boell.org/en/2021/10/13/policies-and-measures-counter-disinformation-germany-power-informational-communities.
8   I discuss these in *Discriminations*.
9   See – for one example (the literature is vast) – Wolfgang Dietrich, Josefina Eachavarría Alvarez and Norbert Koppensteiner (eds), *Key Texts of Peace Studies* (LIT Münster, 2006).

NOTES

Appendix II

1 Reference to committee: Doc. 15337, Reference 4606 of 27 September 2021.
2 Draft resolution adopted unanimously by the committee on 11 September 2023.
3 Doc. 15337.
4 See, for example, Resolution 2369 (2021) 'The Assembly's vision on the strategic priorities for the Council of Europe'.
5 'Reykjavík Declaration, United Around Our Values', Reykjavík Summit of the Council of Europe, 16–17 May 2023.
6 Europol, Terrorism Situation and Trend reports (TE-SAT) from 2007 to 2021.
7 European Commission Directorate General for Migration and Home Affairs, 'Contemporary Violent Left-wing and Anarchist Extremism in the EU: Analysing Threats and Potential for P/CVE', 2021.
8 Council of Europe Committee on Counter-Terrorism, 'Report on Emerging Terrorist Threats in Europe', 7 September 2022.
9 Idem.
10 European Parliament, 'Right-wing extremism in the European Union', Policy Department for Citizen's Rights and Constitutional Affairs, Directorate-General for Internal Policies, May 2022.
11 Idem.
12 P. Wilkinson, 'Violence and terror and the extreme right. Terrorism and Political Violence', 7(4), 82–93, 1995.
13 Idem.

14 P. Castelli Gattinara, E. Leidig, and J. Aasland Ravndal, 'What characterizes the far-right scene in Europe and beyond?', Center for Research on Extremism (C-REX), 7 September 2020.
15 'Understanding the far-right landscape', Centre for research and evidence on security threats (CREST), 14 July 2017.
16 Council of Europe Committee on Counter-Terrorism, 'Report on Emerging Terrorist Threats in Europe', op. cit.
17 'Right-wing extremism in the European Union', op. cit.
18 Resolution 1344 (2003) 'Threat posed to democracy by extremist parties and movements in Europe'.
19 P. Norris, R. Inglehart, 'Cultural Backlash', 2019.
20 Comité R, 'Enquête de contrôle sur la manière dont les services de renseignement assurent actuellement le suivi de la menace posée par l'extrême droite en Belgique, ainsi que le rapport aux autorités', 19 January 2021, p. 23.
21 European Commission, Expert Opinion, 'Violent Right-Wing Extremism in the Western Balkans', July 2022.
22 ECRI, 'Statement on preventing and combating ultra-nationalistic and racist hate speech and violence in relation to confrontations and unresolved conflicts in Europe', March 2021.
23 UNODC, 'Manual on Prevention of and Responses to Terrorist Attacks on the Basis of Xenophobia, Racism and Other Forms of Intolerance or in the Name of Religion or Belief', 2022, p. 3.
24 According to a report from Freedom House, far-right groups supporting violence or the threat thereof are also growing in prominence and sophistication across Eurasia, with serious implications for democratic development in the region.
25 Council of Europe Committee on Counter-Terrorism, 'Report on Emerging Terrorist Threats in Europe', op. cit.

NOTES

26 UNDP, 'From pilots towards policies: utilizing online data for preventing violent extremism and addressing hate speech', 13 May 2022.
27 See Executive summary of the Conference organised by the CDCT, in collaboration with the German Federal Foreign Office, 3–4 November 2022, Strasbourg.
28 Idem.
29 Geneva Centre for Security Policy, 'Strategic Security Analysis', July 2020.
30 United Nations, 'Report of the Secretary General', A/77/266, 3 August 2022.
31 'Council of Europe Counter-Terrorism Strategy (2023–2027)', 8 February 2023.
32 Resolution 1754 (2010) 'Fight against extremism: achievements, deficiencies and failures'.
33 Resolution 2275 (2019) 'The role and responsibilities of political leaders in combating hate speech and intolerance'.
34 Resolution 2443 (2022) 'The role of political parties in fostering diversity and inclusion: a new charter for a non-racist society'.
35 European Commission, Radicalisation Awareness Network 'Between extremism and freedom of expression: Dealing with non-violent right-wing extremist actors', 2021.
36 United Kingdom, House of Commons, 'Extreme Right-Wing Terrorism', 13 July 2022.
37 G. Capoccia, 'Defending democracy: Reactions to political extremism in inter-war Europe', 2001.
38 C. Miller-Idriss, 'Strengthening democracy is the key to preventing far-right extremism', Institute for Global Change, 30 April 2021.
39 OECD, 'Transparency Reporting on Terrorist and Violent Extremist Content Online', No. 334, 2022.

40 Recommendation CM/Rec(2022)16 of the Committee of Ministers to member States on combating hate speech, 20 May 2022.
41 ECRI, General Policy Recommendation No. 15 on combating hate speech, 2015.
42 Resolution 1308 (2002), 'Restrictions on political parties in the Council of Europe member states', 18 November 2002, para. 11.
43 European Commission for Democracy through Law & OSCE Office for Democratic Institutions and Human Rights, 'Guidelines on Political Party Regulation', Second Edition, 2020, 50.
44 V. Tsagkroni, 'Registered, Banned and Excluded: Thoughts on Mobilisation and Exclusion of Far-Right Parties', *GPSG Pamphlet No 7: First Thoughts on the 21 May 2023 Election in Greece*, May 2023.
45 Bundersverfassungsgericht [Federal Constitutional Court of Germany], 2 BvB 1/13 (17 January 2017).
46 J. Hogan, 'Analyzing the Risk Thresholds For Banning Political Parties After NPD II', German Law Journal (2022), 23, pp. 97–116.
47 Guidelines on Political Party Regulation, op. cit.
48 European Court of Human Rights: *Gorzelik and Others v. Poland* [GC], Application No. 44158/98, judgment of 17 February 2004, paragraph 95; *Sidiropulos and Others v. Greece*, Application No. 26695/95, judgment of 10 July 1998, paragraph 40; *Tebieti Mühafize Cemiyyeti and Israfilov v. Azerbaijan*, Application No. 37083/03, judgment of 8 October 2009, paragraph 78.
49 Council of Europe Counter-Terrorism Strategy (2023–2027), op. cit.

NOTES

50 'Strengthening democracy is the key to preventing far-right extremism', op. cit.
51 Committee of Ministers, CM(2015)74-addfinal, 125th Session of the Committee of Ministers, Brussels, 19 May 2015.
52 'Extreme Right-Wing Terrorism', op. cit.
53 Council of Europe, Reykjavík Declaration, 'Reykjavík Principles for Democracy', May 2023.

INDEX

accelerationism 63–4
accountability 12, 91
Alliance for Progress programme 77
Amazon 34, 42, 44, 46–7, 131–2
Amnesty International 49
anarchism 163–4
antitrust 132
Apple 131–2
Applebaum, Anne 95–7
arms and arms trade 70–3, 160
artificial intelligence (AI) 134–5
Atlas Network 60–1
AUKUS 126
authoritarianism 4–5, 6, 74–106, 112, 117, 138, 144, 161, 162, 237–8n42
    advance obedience 94–5
    and anarchism 163–4
    benign authoritarianism 84–6
    business opportunities 50
    centrist politics 82
    civil disobedience 100–1
    collaboration between autocracies 96–7
    and development aid 77–8
    development stages 102–4
    elections, use of 79
    expansionism 98–9
    'halfway' arrangements 101
    and human rights 49–50
    leaders being above the law 141
    opposition to 105–6
    personal experience of 92–4
    return to serfdom 149–52
    reversal in democratisation 79–81
    rights and liberties 87–90
    and the rule of law 83, 86, 87–92, 102

spread of misinformation 103–4
surveillance 92–6
violence 104
autocracy 79, 83–4, 95–6
automation 52–3
Ayer, A. J. 93–4

Bakunin, Mikhail 163
Bangladesh 100–1
Bannon, Steve 69–70, 80–1, 97
Bartels, Larry M. 101–2
Bauer, Michael W. 56
Ben-Ghiat, Ruth 79, 95–6
Bezos, Jeff 44, 46
Biden, Joe 122–3, 175–6
Brennan Center for Justice 167
Brexit 43, 47, 61, 113, 114, 117, 176–7, 249–50n3

Cameron, David 176
capitalism 1–2, 5–6, 39–40, 51
   surveillance capitalism 94–5
centrist politics 82
'The Challenge off Far Right Ideology to Democracy and Human Rights in Europe' (report) 136, 138–42, 178–217
   challenge of far-right ideology to common values 203–5
   conclusions of the report 215–16
   cultural-societal responses to far-right extremism 211–15
   defining far right extremist ideology 192–5
   draft resolution 180–8
   drivers and trends of far-right extremism 195–7
   explanatory memorandum 188–92
   far-right ideology mainstreamed 201–3
   hate speech 207–8
   legal responses 206–15
   online extremist environment 200–1, 208, 214
   restrictions on political parties 209–11, 215
   scope of the report 190–2
   tackling the threat of far-right ideology 205–7
   violent far-right extremism 197–200
China 2, 4, 32, 37, 52
   attempts to destabilise older democracies 118–19, 122–3
   authoritarianism 92–4, 98, 103–4, 117
   Belt and Road Initiative 80, 116
   claims to be a democracy 119, 123–4, 125–6, 127, 129–30
   Confucius Institutes 111, 115
   criticism of the US 124, 126–8
   economic influence 115–17

INDEX

economic power and social/political control 79–80
and Hong Kong 129
human rights record 128–9
serfdom 150
shaping world public opinion 111–13, 115–16
Special Economic Zones (SEZs) 57, 58
whole-process people's democracy 123–4, 125–6
Citizens United v. Federal Electoral Commission 166–7
civil liberties 3, 6, 14, 46, 83, 86, 102, 108, 112, 130, 131, 135, 137, 145–6, 154
as a hard-won achievement 147–50
threats to 137
collective, the 11–12, 14, 123, 126
Committee on Political Affairs and Democracy to the Parliamentary Assembly of the Council of Europe, 'The Challenge off Far Right Ideology to Democracy and Human Rights in Europe' 136, 138–42, 178–217
constitutions 171, 172
constitutional imperative 155–6, 159–62
constitutional monarchy 15

North Korea 165–6
principal features 165
Russia 119, 120
United States 16–17, 22–4, 159, 160
consumerism 42, 150, 164
Convention for the Protection of Human Rights and Fundamental Freedoms 185
Convention on Cybercrime 185
Council of Europe 75, 136, 179, 180, 181–2, 189
Covid-19 pandemic 34–5, 37, 43, 131–2, 139, 195, 201, 204

defence industry 70–3
demagogues 83
democracy 142
benefits of 3
current condition of 1–3, 144, 146
defensive democracy 141–2, 206
definition 9–11
and development aid 77–8
direct democracies 15–17
distinguishing between undemocratic and unrepresentative 30
increase in democratization after 1945 74, 76–7
liberal democracy 135–6, 150
people, notion of 9–10

republican democracy 12,
    14–15, 19, 24–5, 31,
    32–3, 156, 168–9
responsiveness to social and
    economic diversities
    12–13
reversal in democratisation
    79–81
Summit for Democracy
    122–3
synonymity with rule of law 91
as a term ix–x
Diamond, Larry 100

education 135, 142, 182–3, 184,
    186
elections 1, 17–18, 21–2, 27–8,
    175
and authoritarianism 79
campaign donations 39,
    166–7
candidates, choice of 157–8
enfranchisement 10
interference with 113–14
observers 76
'one last democratic vote'
    concept 149
plurality voting 10–11, 17,
    20–2, 146, 147, 172,
    175
proportional systems 147,
    155, 157, 165, 169, 170,
    171, 172
voters' and media audit of
    government
    performance 166

Enlightenment 149–52, 162
eugenics 66–7
European Commission Against
    Racism and Intolerance
    (ECRI) 197, 209
European Convention on
    Human Rights (ECHR)
    28, 197
extremism 136, 138–43, 180–9,
    191, 216
challenge off far-right
    ideology to common
    values 203–5
cultural-societal responses
    211–15
defining far right extremist
    ideology 192–5
drivers and trends of far-right
    extremism 195–7
far-right ideology
    mainstreamed 201–3
legal responses 206–15
online extremist environment
    200–1, 208, 214
tackling the threat of far-right
    ideology 205–7
violent far-right extremism
    197–200
ExxonMobil 47

Facebook see Meta
factionalism 13, 19, 20, 31,
    146–7
fascism 83–4, 138
federalism 19, 169
financial aspects 34–73

INDEX

2008 crash 37, 38–9, 139
arms trade 70–3
austerity measures 82, 99, 139
bail-outs 37
developing economies and multinational businesses 56–7
government disempowerment by multinational businesses 42–4, 53–4, 56–7, 67–8
labour flexibility 41–2
movement conservatism 68–70
national debt (US) 37
privatisation 36, 63, 64
quantitative easing 38
Reaganomics 35–7
regulation and government spending 35–7, 38–9
and social strife 41–2
Special Economic Zones (SEZs) 57–64
taxation 41, 43–4, 55, 165, 173
and the technological revolution 51, 53–4, 56–7
Fisher, Anthony 60
Five Eyes 126
free market concept 137
Freedom House 48–9, 50, 56
Fukuyama, Francis 134

Gaza 50
Gingrich, Newt 69

globalisation 52–3
GNH (gross national happiness) 164
Google 131–2
government
  accountability and transparency 12, 91
  bullying, bribery and blackmail 167
  consent of the people notion 156–7
  constitutional imperative 155–6, 159–62
  devolution 169–70
  discretionary and emergency powers 159
  institutions 156, 158–9, 165
  interests of the people 162–3
  legitimacy of 11, 12, 14, 30
  and multinational businesses 40–4, 53–4, 56–7, 67–8
  necessity for making policy choices 153–4
  political donations, regulation of 166–7
  politicisation of 13
  populist government 55–6, 68, 81–3, 99–100, 101–3, 145
  purpose of 152–5, 158–9, 160, 163, 164, 165, 171
  representation system 156–8
  right to good government 158
  separation of legislature and executive 167–8

voters' and media audit of government performance 166
Greenspan, Alan 63

Haidt, Jonathan 110
Hailsham, Lord 29
Hamas 50
Hamilton, Alexander 16
Han Fei 84–5, 86
Hasina, Sheikh 100–1
hate speech 103, 108–9, 119, 132, 134, 136, 139, 141, 179, 181, 182, 184–5, 186, 187, 202, 207–8, 216
Hitler, Adolf 68, 102
Hong Kong 129
human rights 7, 28, 47–50, 67, 78, 128–9, 145–6, 154, 171, 180, 211
  as a hard-won achievement 147–50
  undermining of 205
Hungary 49, 102, 103–4, 105

immigration 2–3, 54–5, 81, 82, 95, 100, 103–4
India 49, 78
individual freedom/rights 3, 4, 5, 6, 14, 170
Intelligence and Security Committee (UK) 114
International Covenant on Civil and Political Rights 75
International Covenant on Economic Social and Cultural Rights 75–6
International Trade Union Confederation (ITUC) 46–8, 50
internet 6–7, 108, 119, 172, 187
  antitrust 131–2
  artificial intelligence (AI) 134–5
  control of information 132–3
  middleware 134–5, 171–2
  online extremist environment 200–1, 208, 214
  regulation of 132, 134
  use by violent extremists 198–9
Iran 96, 97
Israel 50

Kay, John 42
Kennedy, John F. 77
Kurz, Mordecai 51, 52–4

Labour Party 43–4
Lammy, David 249–50n3
legitimacy, of government 11, 12, 14, 30
Lincoln, Abraham 9
Livy 158
Locke, John 27

machine politics 13
Madison, James 7, 13, 18–19, 22, 146, 150
Madoff, Bernie 38, 39
Maduro, Nicolás 97–8
MAGA 53

INDEX

majoritarianism 13–14
market power 52–3
media outlets 31–2, 166, 168, 203
Meta 108, 110, 131–2, 134, 172
middleware 134–5, 171–2
migration *see* immigration
Modi, Narendra 49
The Movement 70, 80–1, 97
movement conservatism 68–70
multinational businesses 2, 34, 172–3
   authoritarian regimes 50
   benefits of 45–6
   in developing economies 56–7
   disempowerment of government 42–4, 53–4, 56–7, 67–8, 144
   and human rights 47–9
   immunity from justice 46–7
   social aspects 41–2
   support for far right political movements 46, 47, 53–4
   tax havens 41, 173
   technological revolution 51, 53–4, 56–7
   wealth 40–1
Musk, Elon 39, 44, 46, 47, 64–5, 133
Myanmar 49–50

National Endowment for Democracy 111
nationalism 81, 170
NATO 117–18, 122, 126
Nazism 66, 87–8, 149
New York Times 68–9
North Korea 94, 96, 165–6
Nuremburg Laws 87–8

Obama, Barack 21
oligarchy 31
Open Society Foundations 81
openDemocracy 71
Orbán, Viktor 49, 102
Organization of American States (OAS) 75, 76

partisanship 110–11, 145, 146–7
party politics/political parties 144–5
   authoritarian aspects 146–7
   manifestoes 31
   party line 31–2
   restrictions on 209–11, 215
people, notion of 9–10, 12–13, 18, 145, 152–3
Pew Research Center 75
Plato 18, 66
Plymouth and South Devon SEZ 59
polarisation 110–11, 213, 216
police forces/armed forces 183, 199–200, 221–2n13
Population Wellbeing Initiative 65
poverty 2–3, 24, 37, 42, 45, 64–5
power 1, 11, 25–6, 151–3

sharp power concept 111–14
presidencies 15, 21–2
privatisation 36, 63, 64
pronatalism 65
propaganda 99, 103–4, 111, 115, 141, 184
Próspera 60, 61–3, 64, 66
protectionism 55
Putin, Vladimir 97, 98, 119–20, 121–2

Quad 126
Quintus Fabius Maximus Verrucosus 85–6

racism 81, 136, 170, 178, 179, 181, 182, 202
Rand, Ayn 62–3
Reagan, Ronald 35–6, 37, 63, 68
referendums 15–16, 176–7
republicanism 12, 14–15, 19, 24–5, 31, 32–3
Ressa, Maria 105
Roe v. Wade 21
Roman Empire 85–6
Romer, Paul 61
rule of law 3, 6, 14, 21, 67, 83, 86, 87–9, 102, 128, 130, 145–6, 154, 158
  and authoritarianism 83, 86, 87–92, 102
  as a hard-won achievement 147–50
  justice 91–2
  and moral questions 89

principles and procedures 89–91
  protecting rights and liberties 89–90, 91
  and rule by law 88, 90, 91
Russia 96–7, 98, 103–4, 109
  attempts to destabilise older democracies 117–19, 122
  Constitution 119, 120
  interfering with elections 113–14
  reautocratisation 119–22
  shaping world public opinion 111–13

scientific advances 150–1
sexism 81, 82
Seyidov, Samad 136, 138–42, 188–92
sharp power concept 111–14
Singapore 79
Singham, Shankar 60–1
Snyder, Timothy 94
social justice 6, 154–5, 164, 170
social media 2, 6–7, 54
  hate speech 103, 108–9, 119, 134
  middleware 134–5
  online extremist environment 200–1, 214
  personal attacks 109
  and privacy 94–5
  propaganda uses 99, 103
  threat to democracy 109–10

use by violent extremists 198–9
Soros, George 81
sovereignty ix, 27–8, 29
Special Economic Zones (SEZs) 57–64
Starmer, Keir 249–50n3
sterilisation, enforced 66–7
Stockholm International Peace Research Institute (SIPRI) 71
subversion 99, 117
Sun Tzu 99
surveillance 92–6

Tax Justice UK 43–4
taxation 41, 43–4, 55, 165, 173
Techcrunch.com 65
Teeside Freeport project 59
terrorism 107–8, 138, 180, 181, 185, 186, 191–2, 197–9
Thatcher, Margaret 35, 37–8
Thiel, Peter 60–1
totalitarianism 84
Towards the Light 147
trade unions 37–8, 41, 46–8
Trump, Donald 17–18, 21, 39, 44–5, 46, 53, 55, 95, 102, 141, 155
  authoritarian trends 103, 131
  convicted felon 18, 141, 172
  expansionist policies 98
  movement conservatism 68–9

Twitter 108, 131–2, 133, 172
tyrannies 3–4, 85–6, 94

Ukraine 96, 98, 118, 122
UN Sustainable Development Group 78
United Kingdom
  bullying, bribery and blackmail in Parliament 167
  elections 20–1, 27–8, 113–14
  House of Commons 25, 27–8, 30
  House of Lords 26–7, 30, 222n14
  National Health Service 63
  parliamentary sovereignty 27–8, 29
  power of the Crown 25–6
  Special Economic Zones (SEZs) 58–9, 60–1
  Supreme Court 28–9
United States
  checks and balances system 19
  China's criticism of 124, 126–8
  Constitution 16–17, 22–4, 159, 160
  economic success 23–4
  elections 17–18, 21–2, 175
  Electoral College 17–18, 21–2
  House of Representatives 17, 20, 30
  judiciary, political nature of 21

private provision of social welfare, health and education 138
right to bear arms 22–3, 160
Senate 17, 19, 21, 30
society 23–4
Supreme Court 19, 20, 21, 53, 66, 124–5, 166–7, 175
Universal Declaration of Human Rights 75–6

Venezuela 97–8, 130, 150
Venice Commission 142, 209–10
violence 104, 136, 138, 139, 181, 184, 193–4, 197–200
voting *see* elections

Washington Post 44, 46
wealth 2, 7, 164
 of billionaires 34–5, 44–5, 52, 130, 165
 monopoly wealth 51–2
 multinational businesses 40–1, 44, 173
 and power 152
Westminster model xi, 32–3, 167–8
Wikipedia 134

xenophobia 81, 136, 170, 178, 181
Xi Jinping 80, 127

Yarvin, Curtis 68–9

Zuboff, Shoshona 95

A. C. Grayling is the Founder and Principal of the New College of the Humanities at Northeastern University, London, and its Professor of Philosophy. Among his many books are *The God Argument, Democracy and Its Crisis, The History of Philosophy, Who Owns the Moon?* and *Discriminations*. He has been a regular contributor to *The Times, Guardian, Financial Times, Independent, Economist, New Statesman, Prospect* and *New European*. He appears frequently on radio and TV, including BBC *Newsnight* and CNN News.

ALSO BY A. C. GRAYLING

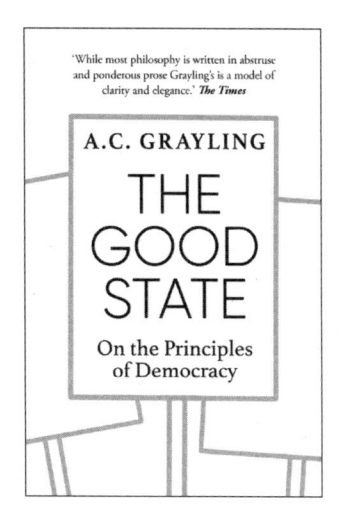

A.C. GRAYLING

THE GOOD STATE

On the Principles of Democracy

'While most philosophy is written in abstruse and ponderous prose Grayling's is a model of clarity and elegance.' *The Times*

The foundations upon which our democracies stand are inherently flawed, vulnerable to corrosion from within. What is the remedy?

As democracies around the world show signs of decay, the issue of what makes a good state, one that is democratic in the fullest sense of the word, could not be more important. To take just one example: by the simplest of measures, Britain cannot claim to be truly democratic. The most basic tenet of democracy is that no voice be louder than any other. Yet in our 'first past the post' electoral system, a voter supporting a losing candidate is unrepresented, the winning candidate frequently does not gain a majority of the votes cast.

This is just one of many problems, all of which demonstrate our need for democratic reform. A. C. Grayling makes the case for a clear, consistent, principled and written constitution, to urgently address the imbalance of power between government and Parliament, imposing fixed terms for MPs, introducing proportional representation and lowering the voting age – to ensure the intentions of such a constitution could not be subverted or ignored.

ALSO BY A. C. GRAYLING

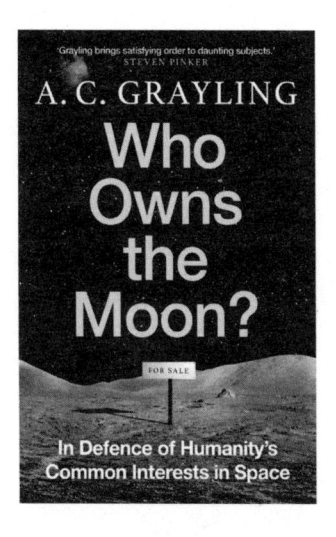

As the world's superpowers and corporations jostle for control in space, A. C. Grayling asks: who *really* owns our planet?

Silicon for microchips; manganese for batteries; titanium for missiles. The moon contains a wealth of natural resources. So, as the Earth's supplies have begun to dwindle, it is no surprise that the world's superpowers and wealthiest corporations have turned their eyes to the stars. As this new Space Race begins, A. C. Grayling asks: who, if anyone, owns the moon? And what do those superpowers and corporations owe to Planet Earth and its inhabitants as a whole?

From feudal common land, through the rules of the sea, to the vast, nationless expanse of Antarctica, Grayling explores the history of the places which no one, and therefore everyone, owns. Examining the many ways this so-called *terra nullius* has fallen victim to 'the tragedy of the commons' – the tendency for communal resources to be exploited by a few at the expense of everyone else – *Who Owns the Moon?* puts forward a compelling argument for a bold new global consensus, one which recognises and defends the rights of everyone who lives on this planet.

ALSO BY A. C. GRAYLING

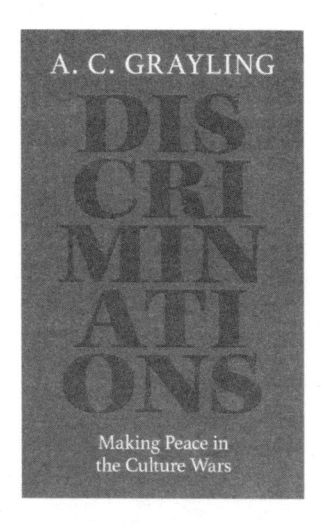

World-renowned philosopher A. C. Grayling explores the messy politics of the 'culture wars'

It seems like we can't talk about anything nowadays… Whether it's war or something utterly inconsequential, the internet is primed for furore. And the results can be horrifying – from online pile-ons and doxing to job loss and, in some cases, death. But how did we end up here?

Nuanced and historically grounded, A. C. Grayling searches for middle ground in an otherwise incendiary debate. Looking at the history of cancellation, from Ancient Greek 'ostracism' through hemlock cups, witch trials and the House of Un-American Activities, *Discriminations* is a timely examination of the state of our public culture and the chilling effect it's having on intellectual discourse.